The Majesty

of the

Woman

by Vernon Tyrone Horton Jr.

DORRANCE
PUBLISHING CO
EST. 1920
PITTSBURGH, PENNSYLVANIA 15238

Dorrance Publishing Co
585 Alpha Drive
Suite 103
Pittsburgh, PA 15238
Visit our website at *www.dorrancebookstore.com*

ISBN: 978-1-4809-5313-0
eISBN: 978-1-4809-5289-8

INTRODUCTION

For so long, the woman has been portrayed as some secular and base being, whose value and divinity is only founded in physical appeal and attraction. I dare to dispel this falsity in *The Majesty of the Woman*. The woman, in today's time, is found in a degraded state, far beneath the royalty attributed to her since inception. I like to refer to her as the "Basket of Life." A basket carries food, which sustains and supports life. In her, we are carried and find rest, as well as sustenance. For nine months, our mothers carry us within the sacred womb, feeding us and nurturing us. We are securely clothed and confined within her flesh, covered from the world that awaits us. She sings to us; she transmits love to us while in the womb, love that pulsates with each heartbeat. While in the womb she talks to us and edifis us about the world that awaits us. While in the womb she whispers forgiveness for any future shortcoming we may have. She manufactures and brings forth great men and women that will serve us and humanity; men and women that will take us from where we are into that which is destined. She gives birth to our freedom fighters, our scientists, our astronomers, our sages, our prophets, and messengers of God. She gave to us men and women that conceptualized ideas of going to the moon; then she later produced those that made it a reality. Conceived in her womb were the men and women that revolutionized medicine and discovered ways to replace failing organs. She carries the hope, aspirations, possibilities, and promises of our future within her womb. When we see expecting women, we should awe at the site of them. She bears the promise of life after ourselves; through her, we are assured. Assured of what? Continuity, another chance at succeeding, and progression through those coming after us. The woman is a thing of beauty, majestic beauty, the rarest of any kind. The man is her protector, he empowers her and leads her as a king leads and upholds his queen. The greatest treasure in any king's kingdom is not his silver and gold, it's not the mass of land and resources under his command, nor is it his army; I say verily, verily, it is his queen and his daughters. Men have lost sight of the invaluable gift we have in women; the gift of having a true and genuine companion and friend. She is there through it all, willing to endure any consequence for being with the man she loves. She exemplifies true strength and zeal. She holds entire families together that would, without her, fall apart. She is both the builder and the mortar. Let us become reacquainted with her and revere her as she should be. This book contains a limited expression of why women are majestic, and it reconnects us with the source and justification of her highness. Do enjoy.

WOMAN

Throughout the ages, many pages have been inked due to her greatness,
To define how divine she is by wise men and sages.
She gives birth; she is the earth; from her, come men of war that rages.
She brings forth those that bring forth cures for disease
that harms and plagues us;
We awe at the stars and adore the sun as it charts the sky in stages.
We weep for the Earth when it's burdened with strife
and seems that hate is contagions,
Such boundless gifts afforded to man by a beauty so profound and ageless!
Yet, what she offers seems to go uncounted,
For such a gift, how could we be so ungracious?
God decreed that man could not live alone, so he gave her as a help-meet,
Only with her could man find completion, and conquer unconquerable feats.
She is the strength in the darkness, the tie that binds, undesirous of any reward.
When the world is too much, she weeps in secret;
in silence, she cries out to her Lord.
She denies herself; she's selfless inside, rarely, if ever, found wallowing in pride.
Man's most suitable companion in whom he can confide;
when all forsake him, she's bound at his side.
Oh, Woman, so majestic, in my mind, I bow to you in reflection,
And for the world, I repent and ask your forgiveness as we strive to embrace correction.
Such a noble being, royal in stature, yet meek and consumed with grace,
I wonder at times, how did we come to this? Instead of honor, we offer disgrace.

I've found my way now because I'm lost in you,
lost in each touch and every glance;
I'm lost in your courage, for when men grow weak,
you never fail in your stance.
I'll hold you high until the sun's flame subsides,
until we love you as we did before,
When you were a Goddess that walked among men,
above anything we'd adore.
The pleasure she gives, the peace she provides,
the gentle utterance of her tone,
The calm of her ways, the softness of her stare,
truly the sweetest things ever known.
Oh, woman, so majestic, so poetic indeed.
I thank God for such a beautiful soul,
I thank God for providing all that I need
to help this half of a man become whole.

Chapter 1
The Value of the Woman

First, it should be well known that the true value of the woman in the deepest sense is literally limitless. Her value has no boundaries, nor can it be measured, only acknowledged, studied, and understood in degrees. Before we go any further, let us define the word value:

> It is relative or assigned worth or importance,
> Monetary or material worth,
> Equivalent worth in money, goods, or services;
> The abstract concept of what is right or worthwhile;
> To consider with respect to worth or importance;
> To regard highly.

Each definition bears great truth and allows us the means to begin to access the value of this being called woman. Let us take favor with the last definition. When we regard anything as "highly," we mentally internalize the vast importance of its worth and nature. We make it our conscious effort and duty to ensure it is handled and protected with the best of care. We maintain it, and if it has a necessity, we provide for it; we do not misuse nor devalue it. The question is: do we see the woman in this same respect? Do we, as civilized men, regard her as highly? I would like to share some very insightful and powerful words that I was fortunate enough to read in an article titled, "Heaven lies at the foot of mother," written by Minister Farrakhan, leader of the Nation of Islam.

> To think of her as only being valuable for procreation and pleasure is devaluing her. To think of her as not being talented or gifted, that she may be an equal sharer in the development of the society, nation or civilization, is to devalue her. To make her a sex symbol is to devalue her. To show her off before the world in an indecent manner is to devalue her. In this world, the man has not given or placed a proper value on the female, and thus, has caused the female to devalue herself. The behavior of our women and our girls demonstrates the thinking of a devalued human. For women to accept to be displayed or kept in an inferior status is to accept the devaluation of herself by the men of this world.

Who would dare disagree with those words? Let's ask some key questions pertaining to what we just read to see if it is irrelevant or reality. First let's ask, is the female portrayed throughout the whole world as an object of sex? Have men given or placed a proper value on the female? Is more attention invested in the intellectual, professional, and divine character of the female, or what she can do to satisfy in the bedroom on a very limited and degrading level? Those not blinded by ignorance will not deny the unfortunate answer to these questions. And how is it that real men, those men of understanding who know the true value of the female, and her importance and necessity to society, stand by and watch the female be treated as though she is only good for physical, perverted pleasure, or to be provided as entertainment, going nude and half nude? Shame on those who lend to this. As far as I can remember, I have always had an untainted and sincere love for women. It deeply troubles me to witness the disgraceful and demeaning way today's women are addressed and presented. It has become the norm now to hear the word "bitch," when males young and old are speaking in reference to women. What makes it even more sad and frustrating is most women now refer to each other as such for nicknames and in idle talk. In my honest view and observation, there are some men who have come to the point where they do not know how to relate to or identify with women without using the illicit "B" word or some other unthinkable title that many wouldn't call the lowest animal. I have often found myself asking, do they have mothers? Were they born of a woman? Do they have children, particularly daughters? Every male, young and old, must be made to understand that every time you call a female the "B" word, you show great disrespect toward your mother, your grandmother, your sister, your aunt, your daughter, and any other significant women in our lives that we love, honor, and enormously respect. It should be against the law to call a woman any kind of name that demeans her, devalues her, corrupts her, and mentally or emotionally abuses her.

Let's go deeper. One of the greatest truths pertaining to the females' existence is that if it were not for women, human beings could not further themselves into eternity. Yes! It is through the female that human beings experience "forever." If the Earth was completely populated with men, because men are unable to reproduce and since death is a universal law, there would come a time when eventually human beings would become non-existent. The law of reproduction is key for survival. So, the presence of woman is therefore a necessity. This means that the world (men in general) have absolutely no respect for the vessel that God uses to allow human beings to embrace the richness and blessings of life and the experience of living. That is the greatest act of ingratitude. The woman MUST be respected and protected. There are many societies and governments in different parts of the world that hold the female of such great importance that she is kept from hearing, seeing, or interacting with anything or anyone perceived as perverse or a danger to her virtue. It is widely known that once the female is corrupted, her offspring will become corrupt as well. Is not the product of something or someone a manifestation of that which produced it? It is vital we understand that the woman is the child's first teacher. She teaches her offspring before birth. While inside the womb, the baby is involved in an involuntary act of intercepting vibes and emotions, as well as feeding from the chemistry and condition of the mother's mind and spirit. The baby experiences, while in the womb, the different emotions and feelings that the mother goes through throughout the course of pregnancy. In many cultures, women are encouraged to read and study more while pregnant. When we begin to take a serious and profound assessment in the deepest sense of the nature of women, we will discover some of the treasures and the gifts that God originally intended for humanity.

The reason we do not behold those gifts and treasures is because of our great disrespect for women. A long time ago I heard the saying, "one man's trash is another man's treasure." A wife was telling that to her husband when she found that he did not want to be with her anymore and asked for a divorce. When I heard the phrase being used in that context, I felt the way that women feel when they are literally dumped and discarded as if they are of no more use, or they find out that the man they love and have earnestly devoted their life to is secretly involved in another relationship. Many women believe that when men cheat, it is because they are no longer as beautiful or as satisfying as they were at first. Some men, through their actions, lead women to believe that after years in a relationship, she can no longer please or provide the desire and attraction that she once did. Truthfully, that's not the case. I believe, in some cases, that men don't know what they want, more importantly need, and most certainly don't know what they have. For centuries, a certain mentality has been perpetuated that the more women you have and have had determines how much of a man you are. It was clear and fortunate that she understood that just because her husband could not see or go beyond the physical aspect of her person and discover that she could please, console, and satisfy in more ways than one (spiritual, intellectual, etc.) that it was not because of her limitations, but his ignorance and miseducation of who and what she is. As said previously, when we begin to study the woman and her nature, we will learn that she is a very special being. In my understanding, she made that statement to him because she knew that she possessed: a boundless and unlimited ocean of love, affection, and comfort that only a man who desired to sincerely love and appreciate her would inherit and embrace. Once a woman gains knowledge of who she is and learns not only her secular, but divine purpose and value, she will guard herself against sexual predators that only seek to misuse her as if she was an invaluable tool that's only good for pleasure.

I am one of those people of whom you could justifiably call a TV fanatic. I love watching television and seeing the great talent of actors and actresses. Just as much, I am immensely fascinated with the brilliance of the men and women that conceive and produce these great films, but on the flip side, I hate to see how the image of the female is reduced to her only being interesting or worth noticing when she has her clothes off. She allows herself to be paraded before the world half-naked and completely naked, revealing her sacred adornments to absolute strangers that have not earned her love. There are young women who sit at home and watch these movies and shows and begin to believe that this is what defines or distinguishes a real woman. The actors and entertainers must realize that they have become the role models of today's youth, and these young adults follow the trends and the fashions that are imposed by what is portrayed on the screen and what they hear. I do not want my daughters to think that to be recognized as a real woman means to dress provocatively and half-nude. A virtuous woman is far more attractive to a man than a loose woman that has no respect for herself and tries to attract men by revealing the sacredness of her body, freely without shame. This is the kind of woman that this world has produced. It hurts me to have a great deal of knowledge concerning the true value of women, and when I go out into the public, I see so many who have absolutely no idea what they are worth in the eyes of God, humanity, and the world. I don't think anything would please me more than to see all women grow into the knowledge of how divine and unique they are and the beauty they provide to this wonderful place called Earth.

Men definitely desperately need to be educated with respect to women in every aspect. It is incumbent that the man be effectively educated on the value and importance of women because if not, the revolution amongst women will rapidly increase, and men in their ignorance will intensify their misuse and mistreatment of them, which will ultimately bring about complete disunity of the two because chaos is contrary to peace, and peace is the nature of the human being. Now, just think about that for a second. God created Man for Woman and Woman for Man. God made the nature of the two to compliment, love, and respect each other, but we are very near the complete opposite of that. The woman is the only suitable companion for man; not only is she suitable, but she is his perfect match. Men, at times, tend to be very egotistical, arrogant, and stubborn. Women tend to be very compromising, merciful, humble, and always willing to sacrifice to make sure that all is well and nothing falls apart, and to secure the contentment of her counterpart. The very character of women seems as though it was designed to tolerate some of the repulsive characteristics of men. What kind of heart must one have to endure things like physical abuse, as well as emotional and mental mistreatment, and still have growing unconditional love for the one who inflicts this pain? Someone please tell me what kind of being is this. To me, women are the most unique and the most mysterious beings. Just to look at a woman and watch her moves, the way she smiles, the way she walks, and the way she talks makes a man wonder to what magnitude of perfection was she created. I have heard many stories in relation to women, as well as the purpose of their existence. Some believe that the woman was a gift from God to the male species for their perfect obedience to God's law and will. Some even believe that women were once angels and God made them flesh and placed them on Earth to help man cultivate and multiply in the Earth. None of these stories have been substantiated or confirmed as true, but they are merely ideas and interpretations of individuals who took time to ponder over the majesty and uniqueness of the woman. Any man who has ever been in love with a woman or still may be would have to honestly testify to the beauty of her character and the sweetness of her personality. The woman has a God-given, divine ability to console the man and put his mind at peace when it is in a chaotic state, just by the soft and gentle whisper of her enchanting voice, and the gentle touch of her fragile hands, she can bring the man from an infuriated state to a calm and serene state. The woman encourages the man to go out and fulfill his dreams and goals and promises that she will be there with him every step of the way, helping him to be successful and prosperous. A dog is not a man's best friend; a dog has never been man's best friend. It is a proven fact that the woman is not only man's best friend, but his truest and equal companion, his helper and aider in his journey to find God and reach his ultimate potential. Time and past experiences bears my witness.

I sit and wonder sometimes, as I ask myself, what is the essence out of which the woman's persona, mind, character, and heart is made of? Because not one can deny that she is a special being. I also sit and wonder exactly what did God have in mind while he was in the process of creating her. There are many secrets that lay within the soul and heart of this being called woman, majestic secrets, ancient secrets, that would give the world a completely different way of looking at women if learned. I implore every reader, man or woman, boy or girl, to go and study other cultures and nationalities to see the various ways each sect, nation, or ethnic group relates to the woman and how they identify her. You should never make the mistake of believing that the way women are viewed and treated in your specific country or state is the same world over because that's just not the case, as in other parts of the world, and in different circles, it is practiced and believed that women are not equal to men but are subordinate to them.

Now, there are some beliefs and sayings that I agree with, and there are many that I disagree with. Even as a young man, I never believed that women were less than or inferior to men. And throughout my life, I never thought for one second that women were subordinate to men and made to serve them. Even in my ignorance, I understood that both man and woman were created to serve and bow down to their creator and in that, they serve one another. What is the source of this great misunderstanding that both men and women have when it comes to dealing with each other properly? It is apparent that both beings are not adequately educated in respect to dealing with one another on a level that would allow them to harmoniously live in a peace with the intentions that God had in mind. Why is this education so vital? What evidence is there to prove that this information is needed? Look at what the producers (mother and father) are producing. Let's look at the ongoing mentality that is carried from generation to generation, only to become more and more dreadful and perpetual in the thinking of those whose responsibility will one day be to evolve and uphold civilization. There once was a time when a man couldn't fathom disrespecting a woman, let along calling her out of her name. You would see men pulling chairs out for women, opening doors for women, and you would find men bowing in honor to women in various cultures.

My great-grandmother, God rest her soul, was always telling me how things were done during the times she lived and grew up in. She told me stories of how difficult it was for a man to win over the woman he was interested in, and how back in those days, men had to honestly earn the love, respect, and trust of a woman. There were courtships set in place that would allow them to go out and spend time with each other in decency and in public. In those days, you couldn't find a woman half-dressed out in public with a man as, of course, that would only tempt them. Now think about it, a woman's body is sacred; a woman is the most attractive creation of all God's creations to man. If a man is in the presence of a half-dressed woman, half of his attention, maybe more, is focused on her body. He never gets a chance to be genuinely interested in her mind, personality, and character because his attention is drawn immediately to her physical body rather than her spirit or mind. Whatever happened to those days when women were so valuable that a young man would literally be interviewed several times by her parents, "mainly the father," before he could begin to talk to her over the phone or take her on a date? What happened? Has the value of the woman diminished? I implore all men to protect women, more importantly, protect the babies; they are precious, and they are indeed the future. Where will we end up if our women continue to produce generations from abused and misguided minds and a corrupt womb? I also implore and challenge all the women of this world and this great nation to protect yourselves, shun indecency, and protect your virtue because this world and especially the field of entertainment has a way of making indecency and wickedness influential and attractive. Look at the greatness that women that have made, monumental and universal changes for civilization. Imagine the kind of human being we could produce if both man and woman were in their right state of mind. Look at the great prophets and messengers of God that came through the womb of a woman to do God's will and help raise the consciousness and morality of the people of Earth. She is God's own special and sacred vessel that he uses to bring forth men and women that are born into the world specifically to bring about a universal change and to make God's will known to those who know not. Look at how significant she is to the creator. How does God feel about the great mistreatment of the woman?

The learned should expediently seek and strive to teach the unlearned, for they will be held responsible for having this knowledge but not sharing it. The duty of any civilized human being is to teach those that are not civilized, for wisdom is a means of survival, and when you teach someone, it is equivalent to saving their life. There is a duty imposed on us by divine law to show the way and teach those that are ignorant. Men must take on the responsibility of teaching and training young mates so that they will not perpetuate the same cycle of ignorance towards women that preceding generations fell victim to. We must teach young men the true greatness of women and SHOW them the true equality among men and women. We must teach our sons of how and why women are so significant to the Creator, as well as to civilization. The greatest nations that ever existed on Earth were composed of the greatest men and women that ever lived on Earth. And the greatest men and women emerged from the womb of a woman. Understand that I have no intention of taking any credit away from men, for I am a man myself, and men do have a monumental responsibility in the reproducing process; but honestly speaking, it is she who carries the baby the full term of pregnancy, as well as bares the intense pain of labor, oft-times alone. And sometimes, she is even left to care for the offspring by nurturing the new life into adulthood by herself. Though the man may forsake her and her child, she is bound by commitment and a God-like quality of unconditional love for her child that no matter how difficult it may be for her, she finds a way, and she fulfills the role of both mother and father. That's a heavy task, but someone must do it. It is she who must go out and play catch, basketball, and football with our young boys in our absence as men, then afterward cook, clean, and hopefully, have enough time to rest for work. In many circumstances, there is no man present for young girls to see how a woman should be treated by her counterpart by observing how daddy treats mommy. Unfortunately, mothers are faced with trying to teach their daughters how to choose the right man. I wonder if God foresaw these things in the beginning? The woman deserves great honor for the burdens she bears and the pain she endures. She has made an unspoken statement that will echo into centuries to come.

I always wondered why God allowed women to undergo these things. Was it to prove to men that their arrogance, pride, and self-proclaimed high stature was unjustified, for the woman was able to endure just as much and work just as hard? Was it to reconnect men with the underlying fact that man and woman were created equal? And most of all, were these circumstances permitted for women to understand their own capabilities and equality? I understand that there once was a time when women were not allowed to vote. I also understand that during one of America's greatest wars, women filled the factories, substituting for the men that had gone to fight for the country. How can any man deem his partner unequal or beneath him when the partner has endured just as much of life's struggle and brings an equal share and maybe more to the table? One of the greatest characteristics that I deeply admire about women is their humility. All throughout the Bible, you read of rich and powerful men, or men that have attained power and wealth, that became arrogant and full of pride, or hard-hearted as if they were the author of their possessions when it was God that granted it unto them. I have yet to read of this personality in the Bible relating to a woman.

What is it about the nature and spiritual make of this being called woman? A woman will walk through hell with the man that she loves, and when he reaches the lowest level of his existence, she will abide with him because she has the ability and the insight to see the potential greatness buried within him; indeed, a God-given, God-centered quality. A woman will even take on the responsibility of providing for her man though it conflicts with her nature, for the man is the provider and maintainer of the woman. But because of sincere and true unconditional love, she will carry her man when he is too weak and not in the position to fulfill his role. I'm not saying that all women will do this, but most of them will, and many have. When a woman truly loves a man, her commitment and conviction to that man is more durable than iron (symbolically speaking). She abides with him through every obstacle, setback, fall, and misfortune, and she helps and encourages him to get back up and continue fighting, for she knows that he is able to succeed. She has a unique heart, a resilient heart that allows her to stand with her counterpart against any enemy, and when all have forsaken him, she remains. In the Bible, you will find that the first person that came to Jesus' tomb after he was crucified was a woman. It was also a woman that anointed Jesus's feet with very expensive oil though she was poor and wiped his feet with her hair (John 12:3). The women that loved and followed Jesus were there with him during his mission, while he was being persecuted, crucified, and after his death, while some of the men that followed him had forsaken him when he persecuted and ultimately crucified.

It is a woman who will love and cherish her man in his most poor and hellish condition, as well as commend and rejoice in him in his most heavenly and prosperous state. She is there when he has nothing, and she is there when he has much materially. She is also there when he has nothing, and there when he has much, spiritually. I am saying all this to say and to prove that in the core of her heart, there lives the true definition of the word love and the real meaning of the words "until death do us part."

In this chapter that I have titled, "The Value of a Woman," my intentions were to bring before each reader facts, beliefs, and experiences that one may grasp and grow to begin to understand the many qualities that women possess, as well as some of the struggles and impediments, and her determination to fight to become an equal in a world and civilization that she helped establish. Most of all, we should ponder and marvel at the great gift that she has that allows man and mankind to reproduce, redeem, and evolve from generation to generation. We live in an age now where society does not reap from this gift because men have lost respect for this divine gift that she possesses, and men have also lost respect for the heart and womb of the woman. Men think that her womb is only for pleasure and enjoyment, when in reality, we are on the complete opposite end of the spectrum. If I may, I would like to share with you six principals that we as men should grasp and internalize, despite our status, religion, or class.

1. Respect the Earth, and it will bring forth good fruit (respectively, there are specific and continual actions involved). Therefore, respect and protect your woman, and she will bring forth and produce great progeny and offspring.

2. Teach and elevate your woman. The only man that desires a foolish and inferior companion is also foolish and inferior himself. For you cannot be both a wise and great man and your woman is contrary, for she is your equivalent second half. She completes your make, and without one another, you're both incomplete.

3. Love your woman with all your heart and soul. When you commit to this sincere act, you will receive the like, but tenfold and there is nothing she will deny you of herself.

4. Always be honest and true to your woman. Never break her heart, for it is fragile and tender. Though you may not perceive it at the time, you will eventually find that not only did you hurt her, but you hurt yourself as well, maybe even more.

5. See your woman as a blessing and treat her as such. Look at your woman and the love that you both share as a blessing and not as something that just happened. Her knowing that you see her as a blessing will unlock in her treasures that have no limit. She will produce beautiful offspring; she will add to your stature and submit to your leadership.

6. Respect her womb, for it is used by God himself to bring forth great spiritual, secular, and moral leaders unto the world that will, through God's determination cause universal change and produce other great men and women through their influence, teachings, and example. And through her she causes both of you to live throughout the ages.

These principles should only be considered the basis or foundation on which we should begin to build a new-found relationship with all women in our lives, be it our sister, mother, cousin, wife, aunt, grandmother, or friends. This process must start first within the household with those of us that are fathers and husbands. We must treat our wives and daughters differently, and we must teach ourselves and our sons differently based on a completely new perception and understanding of women, rooted in spirituality in relation to the Creator. To all of the mothers and sisters in the world, sound the trumpet of revolution. You must reinforce the fact that women are the mothers of civilization. What ever happened to that good old "if you disrespect one woman, you disrespect all women" mentality that used to be so prevalent? What happened to "if you call one woman a 'B,' you call all women 'B's"? There once was a time when these despicable things that we witness today with how men talk to and treat women in such a vulgar and repulsive manner would have, by no means been tolerated. Why is this behavior acceptable now? What has changed? More importantly, has the value of the woman changed? Maybe her value and importance has changed, to the foolish so-called men, but verily, verily, I say unto you that the woman is indeed both precious and sacred in the eyes of the Creator. Let me ask you, if we wanted to produce a new world and a new reality full of righteousness, by what means are we afforded to bring about such a desire? The only way such a reality could come about is through the woman. Once the woman comes into complete submission to God, and God's will, her mind will be submerged and entwined in righteousness, morality, peace, love, and the desire to see mankind become upright and move forward based on all that God desires. When her being and mind is in this state and she becomes impregnated by a like-minded man, her womb will produce a child that is the exact reflection of her mind and heart, and if properly reared, that child will continue the process, affecting all that he/she encounters.

A prophet is only one individual that God selects to go unto the world, and unto a people to teach them and influence them into the proper way of life. God first teaches and gives spiritual life to the servant before sending the servant with a message to uplift humanity. Now, this servant is not fashioned after those whom he is sent to; he has been refashioned by God then sent among those that are in need to ultimately get them to submit to the process that will make them like the servant, a servant to their Lord and pleasing in

His (God's) sight. Eventually, they too will take on that same mission. Everyone that the prophet comes in contact with may not convert, but they are indeed affected in some way and they will begin to think on a higher plane than previously. This is the power of a righteous man in submission to God, he has the ability to affect change in those whom he comes in contact with. But this upright man could not be, and would not exist, if it were not for the majestic and sacred womb of the woman. Once we truly and sincerely begin to realize how valuable the woman is, we must recognize that she is much greater than that. The time has long past that women must know themselves and edify themselves of who they are. There is so much wisdom and so many beautiful secrets wrapped up in women that they can teach their sons, and that would allow them to see that perfect man that they always dreamed of seeing. How about, for a change, we all start teaching our children and give the sitter "Mr. Television" a permanent vacation. That television can be very toxic to the growth and development of young minds.

Now, let's look at the six principles before we move forward. The first principle is "Respect and protect your woman." Women would first respect and protect themselves, that automatically distinguishes them as women who are aware of their self-worth. Men can immediately identify a woman of virtue and respect, trust me! You are your first line of defense against anyone seeking to mislead or misuse you. By you protecting yourself first, you will avoid the wrong places and the wrong crowds, where usually you would encounter the wrong influences: When the woman conducts herself in a disrespectful and unvirtuous manner, men observe this pattern of behavior, and this becomes the means by which he begins to relate to you and with you. Nevertheless, men should hold respecting and protecting their woman as one of their highest priorities!

The second principle is "Teach and elevate your woman." I was always taught that when one seeks knowledge and embarks on a journey to learn, the knowledge gained is invaluable because it was earned. When women begin to teach and elevate themselves with truth and righteousness, there is no man, despite how much she loves him, who can degrade or define her, regardless of how much influence he has over her. The same wisdom that renders unto man great power is also readily available for the woman's attainment as well. So, by no means should a woman ever be inferior to any man. As human beings, we deal more efficiently with that which we have knowledge of, for your knowing grants you understanding and allows you to conceive and effect solutions where conflicts arise.

The third principle is "Love your woman with all your heart and soul." There is a saying that every woman needs love, and I completely agree. Every woman does need love, but women need to love themselves first with all of their heart and soul. Once a woman truly loves herself, she does not have to wonder or second guess if her man really loves her or not because she would already be accustomed to real love and know how to identify it. When a woman truly loves herself, sincere and true love will be required of the man in her life consistently if he desires to continue being with her. This in turn will mature him in his view of women. When we are incessantly honest and true to ourselves, who can deceive us? In most cases, when a person is deceived, it is because they want to believe what they are being told and misled by. Some men can come along and provide women with a vain sense of self-importance, and boost their ego and pride to the heavens. But, when he lets them down and they realize it was an illusion and a front, the fall is long, and very painful. When women are honest and true to themselves, they become humble, and the humility allows you to see yourself as God does and allows you to see your proper place and standings in this marvelous creation. The woman is of divine royalty, created to occupy the throne of virtue and beauty.

The fourth principle is "Speak words of power to build, and not destroy: A husband must learn to be a master craftsman with words." Why? Because words are powerful and have a lasting effect. Your very words can assist you in gaining your desired results or bring about intense frustration and dissatisfaction. When we speak to our wives with respect and sincerity, they respond with such. Let us use love-filled words that gently convey our thoughts and that also empower and motivate her to want to bring about our desires. If ever you are unsure as to how to address your wife about something that displeases you, always pray and seek counsel from an intelligent source... and remember these words: "A fool with a tongue will always be found building what he hates, and destroying what he loves."

The fifth principle is "See the love you both share as a blessing, and not as something that just happened." Women, when you look at your relationship as a blessing, you allow God to be present, for he is the mortar that holds all institutions together, and his absence is the force that tears them apart. When you cast a divine light on your relationship, you increase the potential of eternal unity, happiness, and success.

The sixth and last principle, but no way in the least, is "Respect her womb." Women, you grant the most repulsive, the most perverse, the most irresponsible, and ill-intentioned men such easy access to your most special and sacred adornment: your womb! You allow men to defile and degrade one of the most precious components of your physical, spiritual, and eternal design. Found in the Bible in the book of Genesis is an order and directive given to the first two beings created by God, to replenish, multiply, and subdue the Earth. Women, how can man carry out this order given by God himself without you? What did God have in mind in the beginning of his creation? I believe He desired that eventually, His Earth would be populated with intelligent, righteous human beings that would submit completely to His will. How important is the woman to God in populating His Earth? Although God created Adam first, according to the Bible, Adam was limited and alone. It wasn't until God created Eve that Adam attained a higher degree of balance and grew closer toward becoming complete. They both grew to understand that they were each other's other half. God called Eve, Adams' "help-meet." Eve had to walk the long road of trials and tribulations with Adam, for he could not endure them alone. Men, honor your woman, she was created for you; and you for her. Not for you to misuse her, but for you to appreciate her and the purpose that she serves in continuing our existence on this beautiful planet. Women, respect your womb, for you are not just man's partner, but you are absolutely Gods' helper as well. A woman should never allow any man to exploit the treasures that dwell within her. A woman should never allow any man to use her womb and her heart for vanity and pleasure that fulfills the sick fantasies of the mind.

Woman, you are a sacred vessel and creation of the Creator; within you lies many mysteries, and you should never allow yourself to fooled around and trifled with. You show a greater disrespect than any man toward your Creator by not protecting and maintaining your sacred adornments. Your womb is the portal by which new and innocent life can experience the beauty of living and making changes, while giving their contributions to humanity that will afford the world with the pleasure of leaping forward in whichever field they grow to master. Your womb is not a play toy; in fact, many prayers have been answered by that avenue. It is a strong stance of mine that the world is in such a horrible condition because the woman's womb and mind has been corrupted. The Earth will not bring forth good crops when it has not been properly cultivated and maintained. Many believe that the human being was created from the physical compositions of the Earth. Bones are believed to of the solids and minerals of the Earth. Our blood is said to be of the liquids of the Earth. Our hair is likened to and believed to be of the grass and leaves, and our flesh, of the earth and soil. Now, if we look deeper, the Earth and the woman possess the same ability to bring forth life and reproduce. Such an intricate connection, which should make this theory a lot easier to grasp. This should help us to comprehend that when the woman (Earth) is in a degraded and debased state, it drastically increases the chances of her offspring being identical with her condition. These words are not futile or empty—look at the emerging generations that are coming of age. They are the by-product of the corruption and deviations of their predecessors, parents, and progenitors. The before-mentioned principles were not just conceived overnight, they were given birth by a longing and sincere desire to see true love, admiration, and devotion practiced by all men towards all women. I ask for all to internalize each principle and extract from each one, the benefits of applying them. Why are principles important and necessary? Whenever we are striving to build something, be it an institution, a business, a belief system, what is required first is a **foundation**. A foundation is the basis and support on which everything that comes after is established upon. Webster's definition for **foundation** is as follows: *1. Something (such as an idea, a principle, or a fact) that provides support for something. 2. A body or ground upon which something is build or overlaid. 3. A basis (as a tenet, principle, or axiom) upon which something stands or is supported.* If we were to dissect the foundation of any establishment, system, or structure, we would find that one of the key components are in fact principles; especially when it pertains to our belief systems and the way we perceive reality.

So, I ask, what kind of foundation do we as men have in regard to our belief systems that allow and compel us to mistreat women as we do? More so, what principles are embedded in our foundation. We need to uproot our current belief systems and ways of thinking, as well as our current foundations. We need to replace that foundation with a new one, and contained within should be the principles noted previously. Once we begin to implement new principles that will be infused into a new foundation, that will ultimately become the bedrock upon which a new institution of thinking and understanding women will be built. We must find a way to incorporate and cement each principle into the thinking process of generations to come, as this is the means by which we will be successful in developing a new foundation. The most vital and crucial constituents of this building process is the woman and her offspring. I couldn't emphasize this fact enough. Before we can even make an attempt to modify the present reality and way of thinking, we have to ask ourselves, "How important is the future?" How concerned are we for the future that awaits unborn and growing generations? How involved are we in helping to create an ideal future those coming behind us? What do children have to look forward to if those that are responsible for helping to create their future are asleep on the job? We must study children and identify the many characteristics they embody. Those that are dangerous and/or potentially dangerous to their wellbeing should be removed and replaced by those that will assist in their evolution of becoming great men and women of morale and principles. I understand that if our children are lost, so is our future; and this is why it is so significant for us to understand the importance of refining, restoring, and re-educating the woman based on proper knowledge. Only through true and proper edification can the woman grasp the weighty role she plays in producing the kind of human being God desires.

When the woman finally realizes who she is and understands the divine majesty that she's wrapped in, the world will witness pure beauty and changes of epic proportions never seen in the world from inception. A woman should always be found studying, as this is the means by which she feeds her offspring wisdom. A teacher cannot teach a student that which he/she has not learned. When you are a learned and wise woman, and a woman of virtue, your seed will be born with the capacity and ability to surpass and evolve the knowledge you possess, stretching it beyond its limitations. You will witness new dimensions and new manifestations of your wisdom expressed and exercised through your offspring. Woman! You are indeed a divine creation. The fate of any civilization is wrapped in the palms of the woman's hands, for the woman has the ability to alter the conditions of the world based on the type of seed she produces. She is the first teacher of the child; it is her who implements the first principles. She shapes, molds, and grooms the mentality of the new life while it is in the process of developing thoughts and perceptions in the womb. Water your seeds with an unlimited abundance of love and, they will in turn water humanity with that same love multiplied by both space and time. However, if your seeds are denied the (natural) love they deserves, your seeds will grow cold and void inside (oft-times), and as a result, they may unleash wrath, hurt, and despair into whatever circle they find themselves in. This may not always be the case; however, it is a prevailing circumstance. One of the most effective ways of understanding any situation be it good or bad, is by studying the law of cause and effect, or causality. This particular law provides clarity and comprehension to most of what we experience in life as a result of what is produced from our own actions. We must put all of our intellectual beliefs, our morals, principles, perceptions, actions, and our understanding of God's creation under a microscope and examine them thoroughly to root out any corruption, if any. We must analyze ourselves to see if we are making an honest attempt to live up to the standards set by God, or if we are merely claiming to, to serve as a means of self-fulfillment and self-importance.

As I mentioned earlier, I have six beautiful children that consist of two boys and four girls. Zaki, my eldest, is a very inquisitive young man. Every question that he asks is an opportunity for me to teach and ingrain the principles needed for his evolution into manhood. Because my son has four sisters, it puts him in a position where he has to practice those principles at a very young age. I as well can monitor his actions towards his sisters and correct that which is incorrect and reward him for actions that are in accord with the proper way he should treat his sisters. The scriptures say that if you train or rear up your child in the way it should go, when it is old it will not depart from it. My son has a very kind heart towards his sisters, and sometimes, he even tries to challenge my authority when I am in the midst of disciplining them. Not that it is correct for him to do such a thing, but I see now that in his heart, there is a deep love and intense desire for him to protect his sisters. He understands that it is his duty to keep them from danger and to assist me in guiding and protecting them. He knows that they are physically weaker than he is. I strive to guide him and groom him with each principle each stage of his development, as well as provide other principles suitable for each stage he advances toward. I admit that for some time the television had more of my son's attention than I did. I wondered often what attracted him to television so much. And I learned that aside from entertainment purposes, the television was providing him with perceptions and a belief system of the world that served as a means for him to make sense of this big picture called life. Children yearn to understand. Their soul craves for an interpreter, and guess what? Mr. Television was satisfying that craving. Although a lot of what they see is fiction, it becomes the basis of how they relate to everything they encounter. I did not want my son to relate to real life based on fiction and entertainment. I constantly occupy his time, and I constantly repeat certain quotes or phrases to him so that he will not fall away from that which I want to be his foundation. My son is a very intelligent young man, and I myself am sometimes surprised at the depth of his knowledge and the degree that he executes what he knows. Nothing would please me more than to see my son grow up to be a vanguard and advocate for women and to be a perfect example of how men should respect and treat women. My first act of making it come true is by being the perfect model.

Inayah, my eldest daughter, has one of the most beautiful and enchanting smiles I have ever seen in my entire life. She is indeed a charmer. She was my first daughter, and she opened inside of me a completely different view toward women. As mentioned earlier in this chapter, I do not understand how any man that has children, especially a daughter(s) could refer to women as bitches, and hoes, and all of the other disgusting titles they use to label women. If this is how men see women, then how do we see our daughters, sisters, mother, aunts, and grandmothers? My daughters helped me to realize how precious the female truly is, and I wondered if it had the same effect on other men that have daughters but still blatantly disrespect, and degrade women. Inayah is a very demanding young girl, especially when it comes to attention, and she wants all of my attention, all of my praise, and all of my affection. I asked myself, why is this so?

Embedded within the nature of the woman is a burning desire for her to be comforted, loved, caressed, protected, approved of, and most of all, valued by the most important man in her life, be it her father or husband. We may ask, isn't the mother able to provide that security? Yes, but these are two different levels, dealing with two different natures. The nature of a young girl compels her to resort to her father or a fatherly figure in such a way as to get a feel and understanding on a subconscious level of how she should be treated by men in general, and the man she will share her life with when she reaches adulthood. The father plays a very critical part in how their daughters perceive themselves. When we as men disregard and neglect our daughters, we increase the chances of her believing that she is not valuable enough or worthy of a man's love. She may feel that if her own father doesn't love her, what man will? Inayah is the kind of child that is very big on being loved and wanting to feel special, therefore I want her to understand that she deserves every ounce of love she has ever received and more, and to never accept or tolerate anyone that doesn't treat her like the princess she is. I know how hurtful it would be for Inayah to have her heart broken and to be treated unlovingly when she demands so much love, attention, and affection from me. She demonstrates the authority of a mother over her younger sisters, and sometimes, I watch her and I imagine her being a teacher and a guide for her younger sisters as they grow older, using the influence that she has over them. I understand that what I teach her will aid me in the principals that I am attempting to teach my younger daughters because of the esteem she has over them. Inayah has an aggressive demeanor and a tender heart. She is my eternal shining star.

Destiny, my second daughter, is my angel. If you have ever heard the expression "daddy's little girl," she embodies those words completely. Destiny tells me at least 40 to 50 times a day that she loves me, and she hugs me at a minimal of 15 times a day, and she kisses me at least 10 to 15 times day. When we are in the house, she follows me from room to room asking me questions or finding some way to make conversation with me. One very important and touching thing that I have learned from studying her is that Destiny is very attentive when I am talking to her. She gives me her complete concentration and eye to eye contact. Even when I am correcting her or saying things that she does not want to hear, she gives me the kind of attention as if I was praising her or revealing a long-awaited gift. This had a very big impact on me because my other two daughters are not too big on listening to me when I'm not singing the song that they want to hear. To some degree, I understand that not only the willingness, but the desire that Destiny shows toward me when I am speaking to her, combined with the unlimited expression of love she showers me with, is born out of a natural need and a natural desire within her heart to portray the vast amount of love she possesses. Also, to receive an equal response and reaction. She wants to be loved for her love. I believe that in her own little way, subconsciously, she bases the value of her love on how I, and others, respond to the love she gives; and how I return it, and to the degree I return it back to her. The soft and tender fragile nature of a woman is revealed to us through our daughters. When we begin to see how vulnerable, compassionate, sensitive, and merciful the hearts of our young girls are, we should understand that those same factors and elements are carried with them throughout their entire lives. They are the evolving features of a woman's nature that contribute to who she is and who she will eventually become. These features are so sensitive that if improperly handled and abused, especially by the men in their lives that they love, it will cause them to become emotionally imbalanced, developing an unhealthy perception of men as well as themselves, and it will rob her of the joys of being a woman.

All of these factors concur with our understanding of why our daughters are the way they are to us, their fathers. In Destiny's eyes, mind, and heart, I am the most important man in the world and in her life, and how I treat and teach her will, more than likely, become the basis on how she relates to and judges all men. I will become the example, or the ruler by which she will measure her potential spouse. Destiny has big, beautiful brown eyes, and she is a very beautiful little girl, and I know that Destiny will grow into a very bright, beautiful, and ambitious young woman. My daughters are an undeserved gift to me, and I am making myself worthy by preparing them and teaching them for the years ahead by being a good example of what a true father, husband, and man really looks like.

Samea, my third daughter... where do I start? Anyone who has children, I'm sure, can understand that there is always one that's your "special one." I named Samea after her mother, Tamea. This little girl is absolutely crazy about me; I could never express or convey in words the beauty of having children. It's like having multiple, different versions of yourself following you around, hugging and kissing you, fighting over who's going to get the most attention. Samea has big, beautiful, glossy eyes, and she looks as though she's always about to cry. She's very emotional and sensitive. Her feelings can be hurt very easily with not much effort. She runs to me when she is scared, and she will literally hold on to me for a long period of time until she feels safe enough to let go. Samea has a very beautiful and soft heart; I oft-times visualize her as being a humanitarian or doctor, deeply affected and troubled by how cold the world can be at times. I think the outside world scares her at times and makes her uncomfortable. When Samea was born, I would literally hold her for hours. The doctors would get annoyed with me because they had to weigh her and make sure she was healthy, and do all the other things that doctors do when dealing with a new born. While Samea was asleep in the nursery, I stood out in the hallway watching her through the window day and night, just falling in love with her over and over again. I am sure that I am not the only father that has experienced this, but I had to share it. When we are dealing with the soft and tender, fragile hearts that our women possess, we must realize that they need strong, fearless, wise, and dedicated men to protect them and assist in elevating them above the corrupt view the world has of them. I promise my daughters and my wife, and all women, that with every breath that I breathe, I will fight to defend, uphold, and perpetuate the majesty of the woman. Samea will always have her own little throne permanently seated in the depth of my heart.

The children that I have acquainted you with helped produce the turning points in my life. They have aided me in my understanding of the majestic and beautiful nature of the mothers of civilization that have been sunken and buried under centuries and decades of the lack of knowledge and disrespect of who the woman truly is. My children have also helped me to realize my duty in helping to restore the value of the woman, and that was to start with myself first. I began to study diligently with a sincere desire to learn about women because at a young age I knew that the woman was much more than how she was portrayed by the world. While the world and television was unveiling her body to profit and entertain, I was studying her, trying to unwrap her mind and discover the beauty and the magnitude of her intelligence. I commissioned myself to learn of her merciful heart. I always wanted to know why women were so compassionate and more in tune with their emotions and more opted to peace than men were. Most of all, I always wanted to know why men (even myself) disrespected women as we did. I mean, seriously, what did they do?

Another very disturbing realization is that the disrespect and the degradation of women has now become a culture and a way of life. This culture and mentality is so powerful and prevalent that some men who are not empathetic to it, will bite their tongue, or surrender to that which they do not believe out of fear of rejection or scorn from their peers. That old mentality of "if you can't beat them, join them" has run its course. All of the great men that we marvel at and strive to be like attained their positions and reputations by standing up in the midst of opposition, ready to sacrifice their lives for what they believed in. Who would dare disagree that the restoration of the value of women is worth our lives in the process of giving back to her the throne that she is entitled to? The following are a set of questions that I asked an 18-year-old young man I was interviewing in preparation for this work. His answers are very interesting and enlightening, do enjoy:

Q1. *Why should we make a collective effort in this process of elevating our women?*
Q2. *What role should the man play? And how important is his role?*
Q3. *What is the proper way for a woman to conduct herself?*

A 1. *We should make a collective effort because it's obvious to see that we all have been affected as a whole by the distressed condition of the woman. We all have mothers and many of us have daughters, sisters, aunts, female relatives, and friends. Those that we love we always desire and wish the best for them. How many of us want to see our daughters being abused physically or emotionally? I feel that if we all participated in this process, the power of our unity and like-mindedness would eventually reverse and overcome this cycle. We would reap the benefits of an elevated and new generation being birthed into the world, with new and righteous ideas, to bring into existence a better reality we all have so long hoped and wished for.*

A 2. *The man plays an awesome role in the elevation of the woman. Older men must first and foremost become living examples to younger men. We must teach and show them the proper way to treat women and help them understand the importance of why we must protect and value the woman. The man's role is to be a guide, a warrior, a teacher, and most of all, a doer. If we do not practice what we preach, we will not be successful. I have realized that once we start this process, our journey will unlock higher realms of understanding and will reveal many things that we once were completely unaware of. The man is the vanguard, and this is the most crucial role one can perform in the act of defending something or someone.*

A 3. *The woman should always conduct herself in an extremely respectful manner, from the type of clothing she wears to the way she speaks and the words she uses. She should never try to attract a man by revealing her body because more than likely that will be all he is interested in. And because it's not the physical that completes and fulfills the eternal and internal desires of the human being, most likely both will eventually separate whether it's a physical or mental separation, because there was no divine or spiritual connection in the beginning. When there is a spiritual and intellectual connection between two people, their relationship has a greater chance of surviving because they are able to fulfill each other's needs outside of the physical realm. Women should always conduct themselves in a majestic and royal manner, always conscious of their value, identity, and importance to both God and humanity. If any woman should find herself in a non-productive relationship where her man does not value nor respect her, out of love, it is just for her to make an attempt to educate him and teach him the wrong of his ways in regard to his mistreatment of her. But if this behavior persists, she should leave him alone and wait for the king to come along that will earn her love and cherish the beauty of her heart and mind.*

Hearing this young man's response gave me a greater sense of hope… and inspiration. The degree of love and passion we have for anything is manifested through how long we are willing to endure and suffer the trials, and the natural hardships to get the desired results. Through our study and edification of the woman, if we are sincere, we will inevitably unlock a natural, divine, and pure love for her; and that love will produce a profound and unbreakable love that will increase so long as we continue the process. Men, honor your woman, love your woman, and in whatever areas you are knowledgeable, teach your woman. You should also allow her to teach you, as there is so much you would understand about her if you would just let her teach and tell you. This is not just some project; this is a journey. Our children should be taught that the misuse and mistreatment of any woman is completely unjustified and will not be tolerated. Our young men must be taught that to be a real man does not mean to have multiple women, or to have her "in check" and make her submissive to him. A real man takes care of his woman, protects his woman, elevates his woman, and gives his woman the utmost respect no matter what the situation may be. Men, show your sons that this defile image of men pimping women and degrading women, making it seem as though they are not valuable and majestic creatures is a false personification perpetuated by those that are completely ignorant of who the woman truly is. Show your daughters through how you treat their mother, and other women, how a real man treats and deals with all women because she's watching and listening to every move you make and every word you speak. Women, elevate yourselves, and when you can't find a man to uphold you, then uphold yourself!

Till Death:
The Beauty Of Marriage,
The Sacredness Of Vows

TILL DEATH

From the time the sun rises until it sets again,
And there is no more light upon the Earth,
Till death, I am yours, you own the whole of my heart,
And it's only for your love that I thirst.
This vow that we have made, allow no soul to ruin;
This bond has been sanctioned by the Lord.
Though we are two, our flesh becomes one;
In this life, you are my greatest reward.
We will stroll down the aisles of a never-ending story;
We will treasure each year that has past.
Of all the things I have done that have afforded me glory,
It's just our love that I pray shall last.
A man shall leave his parents and cleave unto wife,
And a woman shall do the same,
We shall emerge in one another, then share one heart,
We both shall be called by one name.
Let not these words be vain to your mind;
Please believe all that I promise and say.
I want you here by my side through the brightest and the darkest,
Till death we shall live life this way.
They say that happiness resides in two hearts in love;
They say that God is the giver of smiles.
Well, then we must be in love, and you must be from God.
Our love prospers in the midst of our trials,
Like a red summer's rose, we add beauty to creation;
Like the stars, we add brightness at night.
Till death, I will love you, and if loving you is wrong,

Then today, I redefine wrong as right.
My tears would be endless, and my sorrows plenty,
If I had to go one day without you.
If I am a lock, you are my perfect key;
I am one, but what is love without two?
Till death, I will remain; till death, I am your friend.
I cherish the very breath that you breathe.
Only death can take or separate our flesh;
Only death can cause me to leave.

WHAT IS MARRIAGE?

Well what is the purpose of marriage? What makes marriage beautiful? What aspects of marriage are people more prone to consider when considering marriage? Is it the beautiful flowers? Is it an overwhelming desire to partake in such a beautiful experience? Is it the attractive and captivating set-up of the ceremony? Or, do we understand the true precepts (a command or principle intended as a general rule of action), conditions, and expectations of being joined in holy matrimony to the one whom we plan to say **"I DO"** to?

I have realized that in some or most cases, not all, many have taken spirituality out of marriage and have made it into some secular event, more grounded and based in entertainment and emotion. In any country, especially the U.S., where you find more than 50 percent of the television shows, sitcoms, and movies with couples that just live with one another without being married, we cannot be surprised of the tremendous effect it has had on past and present generations. Let us not forget about the T.V. shows with the single men and women that live alone but have very promiscuous (not restricted to one sexual partner) lifestyles, with a variety of different sexual partners. The bachelor and promiscuous lifestyle has become a culture in America and other parts of the world. Why is it that a government as powerful as it is will not use its influence to urge movie producers to promote marriage and family life? An America that promotes and encourages marriage and family will produce a healthy, structured, and more stable America. The answer to this question ties into the actual purpose of marriage. God, whom is the All Wise and All Knowing, would not create marriage, nor has He created anything without a divine purpose. If we study all that exists, we will always find that God creates with extremely wise intentions, having something to do with the balance, stability, perpetuity, and success of man and woman. In order for us to discover the purpose of marriage, we must tap into the spirit of the one that created marriage. Was it really necessary for the All Wise God to even bring such an institution into being? Could it be that man and woman would have been just fine without marriage? Many may say yes because there are indeed couples that share their home, their life, their money, their secrets, and have children that they love, but they are not married. They would say that although they are not married, they have a beautiful family and a well-balanced relationship wherein both are happy and sincerely committed to one another. Well, if this degree of success is attainable in a relationship not governed by marriage, then is marriage really necessary? ABSOLUTELY!

In order for us to understand why marriage is so critical, we must understand what it is and what its purpose is. Now, we all know is that God created man and woman for one another, but why? What is the tie that binds and keeps them together? Is it sex? What is the great bond that this wise master would use to keep a husband and wife together once they are wedded to one another? Is it love? Well, we see people that so call "love" each other walk out on one another continuously when they become frustrated or extremely dissatisfied with certain aspects of their relationship. What was the **reason** or the **purpose** for marriage being imposed by the All-Knowing God? A God whose wisdom and knowledge is supremely perfect! According to Webster's New Collegiate Dictionary, purpose means: Something set up as an object or end to he attained: Intention b: Resolution, Determination 2: a subject under discussion or an action in course of execution *syn* see Intention. To propose as an aim to one's self. According to this same source, marriage means:

> The state of being married b: the mutual relationship of husband and wife: Wedlock c: the institution whereby men and women are joined in a special kind of social and legal dependence for the purpose of founding and maintaining a family 2: an act of marrying or the rite by which the married status is effected; *esp* : the wedding ceremony and attendant festivities or formalities 3: an intimate or close union.

Marriage imposes **divine law** and **divine responsibility** on the bond that is made by the two. **Two of the main purposes for the adjoining of man and woman are to become one with God, and the eventual perfection of them both**. God being the creator of man understood that his creation was not perfect but had the absolute potential to be and become perfect, so in His unlimited and boundless wisdom, He created the woman to assist man in his journey to become perfect and to become one with the Creator. The man (past, present, and future tense) has both awesome and difficult tasks imposed upon him by his Creator. Tasks that require a companion, a partner, a comforter, and a consoler. Someone that can motivate and quiet the restless mind, as well as agitate the soul out of the comforts of complacency. It is the destiny of man to master any discipline he engages, as well as the adversities of life. Man's mastery of anything is directly connected to his relationship with his creator, and his journey of becoming one with his creator is facilitated and assisted by his womb-man! The wife becomes a mirror for her husband so that he may see his hidden impediments (spiritual, mental, physical) that are tucked away and disguised within the vastness of his ego and pride. Many, if not all, recognize that it is the destiny of human beings to eventually become one with God. The man or woman that has become one with God is no longer inspired or motivated by his/her own desires. The man or woman that has become one with God no longer operates with their own judgment, emotions, wisdom, or understanding; they are under the complete guidance and direction of the Supreme Being. The result of being under the complete control of an all wise, all powerful and perfect Supreme Being is perfect decisions, perfect analytical calculations, a perfect and righteous lifestyle, and a perfect understanding of how to evolve and cultivate other forms of creation. Anyone that believes that perfection is unattainable to man doubt the wisdom, the power, and declaration of man's Creator. Perfect: to make perfect: Improve, Refine 2: to bring to final form. Now, let us take some time to really reflect on this definition. Now, I know many will say, "None is perfect but the Father!"

THE UNION OF THE TWO

Genesis 2:18. And the Lord God said, "It is not good that the man should be alone; I will make him an helpmeet for him." We must first understand that one of the primary reasons God created the woman was because Adam was imperfect and incomplete. Although, when looking at Adam's physical make, he looked complete and well-balanced, but his Maker, his Creator, could see deep into the essence of his physical, mental, and spiritual composition and see the imperfections of a marvelous masterpiece. This does not imply that the woman given to Adam was perfect or complete and would in turn show Adam how to become perfect and complete him. How do we know this to be true? Why did God say, "It is not good that the man should be alone; I will make him an helpmeet"? Well, why wasn't it *good* for man to be alone, and what is a *helpmeet*? According to Merriam-Webster's Dictionary *good* is defined as: Of favorable character or tendency 2: Bountiful, fertile 3: Comely, attractive 4: Suitable, fit 5: sound, whole 6: agreeable, pleasant 7: salutary, wholesome 8: considerable, ample 9: full 10: well-founded 11: true 12: legally valid or effectual 13: adequate, beneficial. These definitions are very thought provoking. In the Webster's New Collegiate Dictionary, I found one of the definitions for the word *good* very interesting in relation to this particular topic. The definition is: 1. certain to last or to live. In God saying that it was not good, he was also saying that man was inadequate to be alone. He was saying that it was not suitable, nor was it beneficial, for man to be alone. Man was not whole, nor was it wholesome for man to be alone. He was saying that based on His divine and infinite intention for creating man, it was not legally valid or just for man to be alone. One definition for valid is: Capable of being justified or defended. The man's existence is justified and perpetuated by the connection and interaction of his being with woman. God was confirming that it was not certain that man would last or live if he were to be alone. That majestic being called Woman enables creation and life to multiply and regenerate. It defeats the very purpose of God to create life, without life being able to continuously reproduce itself. It is my humble opinion that, with the exception of our relationship with our Creator, the divine bond of husband and wife is the most magnificent and awe inspiring. When we think about marriage, we often mistaken the beauty of it as that which is brought out through the wedding ceremony; rarely do we anticipate what comes after. Our lack of understanding relative to the nature of male/female causes complications, boundaries, and disparities of enormous proportions. Why is this so? Well, how does one deal effectively and appropriately with that which they have very little or no knowledge of? Would we allow someone that has no knowledge of automotive maintenance and mechanics to "fix" our car? Would we ride on a plane with a pilot that has absolutely no idea how to operate it? Would we allow someone that has never studied medicine to administer medicine to us, perform surgery, or remedy a serious illness? These questions may seem a bit absurd or even silly, but I would say, so do most marriages. A large proportion of why marriages began to fall apart is due to husband and wife lacking that profound, divine knowledge of one another, and how they should relate to one another. We get lost in sex and the physical composition of one another, and when we began to sober from our sexual intoxication, we are left wondering what's left to explore. And because the man, whom Paul described as being the head of the woman (Ephesians 5:23) lacks the essential knowledge and understanding of his woman, he does not know how to mine out of her what's in her that was deposited by God Himself, to justify her as being his helpmeet. The man becomes ever-so impatient with his woman because he does not understand her, and naturally, he does not understand how to deal with and cultivate her.

As men, we sometimes do not understand the natural evolution in our connection with our divine mate. We oft-times expect our presence in the relationship to be sufficient and satisfying to her, and we can be so foolish as to think that being handsome, good in bed, and even giving her material is what maintains the bond between them. When the relationship takes an unexpected turn, due to us not being prepared because we do not understand who she is on a divine level, our reactions are detrimental to the relationship. What unexpected turns am I referring to? Well, as I recall a very close friend of mine saying, "When we first got married everything was perfect at first, then, out of no-where she started COMPLAINING." This is one of the most hated and despised occurrences of men in the marriage. It strikes a devastating blow to his ego and brings the husband down from his high horse into a more realistic realm and says to him, "You have flaws; you are not perfect; you must work on yourself. You have to concede that this woman whom you lead is correct, and you have to submit to her critique of you, your good looks, money, and bedroom capabilities do not adequately satisfy and secure her." If men understood that women are the natural identifiers of our flaws, we would expect at some point for her to begin to act on this quality of her nature, and we would be prepared for the interaction. When wives are not satisfied in every instance, that is not necessarily an indication that she is "divinely right" and we are falling short in our duties. Certainly, a woman may have extravagant desires, just as men do, in some cases more, and it is the husband that has to counter those desires and sway her with reason and logic. What I'm attempting to convey is that it is the nature of man to evolve into his fullest potential in every area of his being. The woman that's given to him by his Creator **helps** him to fulfill this! The help may not always come in the form most appealing to him, but nevertheless, she is man's helpmeet. She helps him to identify his weaknesses (complaining, expressing dissatisfaction, even silence, etc.) she encourages him and motivates him to go further. She helps him with projects; she is a perpetual consultant and confidant. She tends to his wounds while denying her own, and she endures inexplicable pain in child birth that the man may see himself again in his offspring. She cautions him from sin and living dangerously. She studies him, that she may edify him of himself when he can't understand where he's going wrong, and she roots out, with precision, all areas of weakness and insecurity in both the relationship and the family structure and will explain what needs to be done individually as well as collectively to fix it. She is indeed, a marvelous being. Women are very skilled at sensing insecurity. She is designed to pinpoint the flaws and weaknesses of her man, as he may get blinded by his own ego; physical strength, title as "head of house/woman." How the wife introduces these flaws and perceived flaws to her husband is so key and important to their marriage and relationship. If she does it shrewdly, attacking his manhood and sense of worth, she very well may awaken that Leviathan that's buried deep within him that can open up a world of pain, disunity, and disrespect to the marriage. But, if she does it with a gentle hand that's clothed in humility, love, and meekness, though she may encounter some resistance, she will maintain the sanity and tenderness of her relationship.

I often ask married couples which part of marriage they enjoy the most, if it's the event of getting married, or the lifetime of togetherness. We invest thousands of dollars as well as time into making sure the right music is played, the food tastes great, and all the while subconsciously oblivious to the reality of what lies ahead. We even go as far as giving gifts to the ones who participate in this wonderful event. Why do we do this for one day, when what happens afterwards is the second most important commitment we will ever make in our life? A divine contract might I add, with the Lord of Creation as witness. Once this joining of man and woman has been sanctioned by God, a divine directive is then given—"Therefore what God has joined together, let no one separate" (Mark 10:9). Before I continue, I would like to share with the reader one monumental article that is derived from an actual lecture by Minister Farrakhan. The article inspires divine reflection in both genders as it relates to their role and responsibility to/for their prospective mates. So please read, reflect, and enjoy!

In The Name of Allah (God), The Beneficent, The Merciful.
In all of the three monotheistic religions, which claim Abraham as a Father—Judaism,

Christianity and Islam—the institution of marriage is considered sacred because, according to the scripture, it is instituted by Allah (God). **Anything originated or instituted by Allah (God) must be considered by us as Divine or Sacred, and must be respected accordingly.**

Sacred:
Dedicated to, or set apart for, the worship of a deity. Worthy of religious veneration. Made or declared holy. Dedicated or devoted exclusively to a single use, purpose, or person. Worthy of respect. If we do not give due respect to that which is of Allah (God), we offend Him and, from this offense,

a series of offenses take place. Therefore, we must look again at what Allah (God) intended when He instituted marriage among the original parents of the human family. The present view of marriage is so distorted that the relationships and the offspring from such a distorted view becomes a distortion or an aberration.

Distort:
To twist awry or out of shape; make crooked or deformed. To pervert; misrepresent.

Aberration:
The act of straying from the right, normal, or usual course. Deviation from truth or moral rectitude. According to the scriptures, when Allah (God) created the man, He created for him a helper that was *fit* for him.

Fit:
Adapted or suited. Proper or becoming. Qualified or competent. Worthy or deserving.

This teaches us that the woman was made suitable to the requirements Allah (God) had put upon the male as his duty in service to Allah (God). So, the female was made, prepared and qualified to help this man do the job that Allah (God) had given him. In the nature of the man, and from the Divine Instruction given to him, and from the mate given to him, this teaches us something about the selection process for marriage.

Every male and female, when they reach the age of puberty or adolescence may have a physical desire to experiment with sex; however, they may not yet have matured into the knowledge of what work they are to do in life that fits into Allah's (God's) plan for them. Consequently, the male may not know what female is fit for him as a helper in the work of Allah (God). Unfortunately, we allow the nature of attraction and our natural desire for the opposite sex to be the basis for choosing our mates. In doing this, we have violated the very principle upon which marriage should be based. The predicate for marriage has to be a mature knowledge of self and what the self requires as a helper or mate to fulfill a Divine Obligation.

Predicate:

To base or establish. To state or affirm as an attribute or quality of something. To proclaim; assert. The Bible teaches that Allah (God) made the woman and brought her unto the man. In this case, Allah (God) was the ***Perfect Match-maker***, for He made the man; He knew what He put in the man; and He knew what the man would need to complete his make. So, Allah (God) joined these two in marriage and declared that a man should leave his mother and father and cleave unto his wife and they shall be one flesh. This indicates that, if man and woman in marriage are to become **one flesh**, in them shall also be one mind and spirit. This is what presents the difficulty—**making the two of one mind**.

We begin the language of mathematics with the number **one**. We begin our journey into the knowledge of Allah (God) by declaring that He, Allah (God) is **One**.

We begin the real journey of life through the institution of marriage when we declare our desire to become as **one**.

Since Allah (God) is **One**, the universe is one, the only way that marriage can be successful is for the man and woman to strive to become as **one**. For the man to see the woman as an object of pleasure or to further him in procreation is only partially seeing the purpose of Allah's (God's) creation of the female.

The strengthening of the union of the male and the female in the institution of marriage is the best preparation for the production of family. Prophet Muhammad, Peace be upon him (PBUH), said, "**Marriage is one half of faith**." The journey of faith begins when sperm is mixed with ovum. The journey of faith does not end until we become one with Allah (God), well pleased with Him and well pleasing in His sight.

Since none comes to Allah (God), except as an honored servant, Allah (God) has always tried all of His Prophets, Messengers and people severely in their journey toward Him. It is these trials and afflictions that are part and parcel of the journey of faith that makes the reward of that journey so soul satisfying. After completing these trials, we become a soul well pleased with Allah (God) and well pleasing in His sight.

Since the institution of marriage is one half of faith, then similar trials that are experienced in the journey of faith are also visited on those two souls that desire to become as one. After completion of many trials, the two become well pleased in the eyes of each other and well pleasing in the eyes of Allah (God).

How does the female help the male to do the work of Allah (God)?

The role of every male is to do the work of Allah (God). In the Qur'an, the man is made to stand in the place of Allah (God). This means that the work of the man is really the work of Allah (God). That work entails the building of a world that manifests the characteristics or attributes of Allah (God). This world includes a nation, a government, systems of education, economics, judicial, trade, commerce, research, development, science, industry, agriculture and agribusiness. This is the work of Allah (God) to supply the needs of the human being as He has supplied the needs for all of His creatures.

When man assumes the posture of Vicegerent or Khalifah, or one who stands in the place of Allah (God) acting on the Will of Allah (God), then the scripture in the Book of Psalms is fulfilled, wherein it reads **"Ye are all gods, children of the Most High God."**

In all of the work that man is to do in the place of Allah (God), the woman is his helper in forming the nation, the government, the systems; exploiting the gifts, skills and talents of the people in their service to Allah (God).

Each gifted man needs a gifted woman to help him to fulfill the objective of standing in the place of Allah (God). The male and the female should be of one mind in doing the work of Allah (God).

All of this can and will be done when we adopt Allah's (God's) view and purpose for the sacred institution of marriage.

Now, before we delve into some of the implications of this article, please consider carefully the last sentence in the article where it says, "All of this can and will be done when we adopt God's view and purpose for the sacred institution of marriage." We must strive to see marriage through the eyes of the creator that we can cease our disrespect of his sacred institution. We **must** learn of marriage and its sacred tenets. Why? Because when we understand what it is we are embarking on, we will not approach it with disrespect and carelessness. I once heard a quote that goes as follows: "Wise men fear to tread where fools rush in." A wise man/woman will prepare themselves for such a covenant, for they truly know that once wedded, they are joined until death. Those that are wise understand that to rush into anything is dangerous. Two souls that have committed themselves, first to God, then to one another, has laid before them a whole world unrealized, that they will create and bring into existence. Outstretched before them lays a road filled with places, experiences, children, loses, gains, disappointment, laughter, bitterness, joys, dreams, aspirations, wants, and desires, that await them as they stand before each other. With God as their witness as they say, "I do," and they will abide with one another down this path "Till Death." They will experience both separate and collective trials, and they are to aid one another through each trial. Whereas one is strong, he/she are to use their strength to support their counterpart, and with each passing trial that's endured and overcome, the bond grows stronger, and the love deeper. The days that seem colder and suggest that maybe the marriage wasn't meant to be, they are the days to be outdone. Those days, hold each other longer and tighter, delight in both soft and passionate kisses, force "I love you" from clasped lips and a hardened heart. The Creator watches throughout the entire journey to see if both souls were sincere when they invoked his name and cried out for his blessing of their union. He watches from on high! That is how sacred this union is. Husbands, handle your wives like the rose that she is, for she is delicate and fragile, inside and out. She cries a lot easier than you, so be patient and loving toward her, even when agitated. Talk with her more importantly, have deep and intriguing, uninterrupted conversations with her, and make sure she has your undivided attention. Walk with her and stare at her while walking so as for her to know that you desire to pierce the veil of the flesh and go beyond the seen. This is what facilitates and strengthens the desire in her to help you in your duty as Man. Man the provider, Man the protector, Man the sustainer, Man the builder—Her Head.

One of the realizations that I have come to that has been so shocking yet sobering is that most men/husbands do not understand how important our wives are to our successes in life. The more we discover and learn, the more we appreciate the woman. However, discovery holds dear to me, as it reveals the stage that causes so much failure in most relationships. After the smoke of passion, lust, desire, and infatuation clears, and the natural inclinations of the flesh has somewhat subsided, the bride and groom are now being introduced to aspects of one another that were concealed at one time. The likes and dislikes are beginning to brew and emerge. The flaws of imperfection are on display, and selfless adjustments are a requirement to proceed and make progress. Doubts begin to emerge in the minds (possibly), as well as fear. I mean, let's be honest—how does one anticipate the unknown? This is why preparation is so key. The bride and the groom should know at some point in their marriage they will encounter emotional, mental, physical, and spiritual elements of their mates that they are unaware of and unprepared for. Sex does not acquaint you enough to enable you to develop a bond that will endure through the ages of time. Intimate conversations, the exchanging of ideas and the revealing of deep, dark secrets gives way to a bond of perpetuity. Sadly, I've found that many couples that I encounter, either through my work, through social inquiries and studies, both immediate and distant family, do not go out (or stay in) and spend quality time with one another. I was once told by a very close acquaintance of mine, about his relationship with his wife that "wasn't meant to be." I asked why he felt this way, and he replied, "I feel like I don't even know her, and she barely even knows me."

I responded in the humblest manner that, "Maybe the two of you don't know each other."

I then asked what steps he had taken to remedy this challenge in his marriage versus seeking to separate. His reply was one that I hear so often when speaking with couples that are considering separation.

He said, "We go out to the movies and to eat. We do all sorts of things."

I asked him when was the last time they had a deep, intimate talk with one another, where secrets, fears, deep aspirations, and desires were shared. He said such a thing was weak, pointless, and stupid. It hit me at that moment that some spouses are merely roommates; more or less bunk buddies and financial partners, lacking an intimate connection. I'm not implying that the only way husbands and wives can build a true bond is by revealing all of their arcane and inner thoughts to their spouses, but we must be cognizant of the fact that our bond is a deliberate act that is done on purpose and not something that comes about by chance. Husbands and wives are locked in a constant struggle to understand and empathize with one another daily. There are so many barriers to break through, and so many sealed doors that must be opened if there is to be a true oneness in a marriage. I gently chided my friend by pointing out to him that it was not fair to his wife or himself that after 16 years of marriage, they did not know one another. He didn't want to take accountability for the current condition of his marriage, but I opined that as the head of his divine union with his wife, much of the burden falls upon him. He gazed at me with stern eyes of disagreement and disbelief, as he could not believe that I, being his friend and a male like himself, would choose the side of his wife. The truth is I wasn't choosing sides, but was simply

conveying that as men we bear most of the responsibility because our divine ordinances command us to lead. I referred to a passage in the Bible that he was not only familiar with, but could almost recite verbatim. This particular passage is found in **Ephesians 5:23-32.**

> *23 For the husband is the head of the wife, even as Christ is the head of the church: and he is the saviour of the body.*
> *24 Therefore as the church is subject unto Christ, so let the wives be to their own husbands in everything.*
> *25 Husbands, love your wives, even as Christ also loved the church, and gave himself for it;*
> *26 That he might sanctity and cleanse it with the washing of water by the word.*
> *27 That he might present it to himself a glorious church. not having spot, or wrinkle, or any such thing: but that it should be holy and without blemish.*
> *28 So ought men to love their wives as their own bodies. He that loveth his wife loveth himself.*
> *29 For no man ever yet hated his men flesh: but nourisheth and cherisheth it, even as the Lord the church:*
> *30 For we are members of his body, of his flesh, and of his bones.*
> *31 For this cause shall a man leave his father and mother, and shall be joined unto his wife, and they two shall be one flesh.*
> *32 This is a great mystery: but I speak concerning Christ and the church." Verse 24 clearly states that the husband is the head of the wife, and we all know that the head leads the body...*

I asked him, "How and where have you been leading your marriage and your wife?"

He could not answer, and I asked him to not get offended, but instead, to open his heart to what I was saying because I was only interested in helping to strengthen the bond between him and his wife. One of the essential components of leadership and guidance is communication. To lead, to cultivate, to grow, to inspire, to motivate, and to teach anyone requires communication, the kind of communication that leads to and facilitates the development of trust and cohesion. Verbalizing commands and giving directives is not the kind of communication I am referring to. I asked my friend the following questions:

1. *How often do you hold your wife, stare into her eyes with a smile and tell her you love her?*
2. *Do you invite her to store and errand runs?*
3. *How often do you surprise your wife with flowers, candy, or random gifts?*
4. *After a long day at work, do you come home and retreat to mental solitude?*
5. *How often do you initiate holding hands?*
6. *Do you open and close doors for your wife?*
7. *Do you tell your wife how afraid you are of losing her?*
8. *Do you pray with your wife?*
9. *Do you confide in your wife, and ask of her thoughts on the matter?*
10. *Do you and your wife have a mission statement?*
11. *How often do you call your wife when away from her?*
12. *How often do you compliment your wife?*
13. *How often do you serve your wife?*

I will not disclose my friend's responses to the questions, but suffice it to say, he has a lot of work to do. I will say, however, that he was very honest and open with himself in terms of where he fell short in his marriage. It helps tremendously when denial is not a factor in the rebuilding process. Denial will hinder and block all progress. As men, if we do not come to terms with all that we are responsible for (which is just about everything), the fall is destined and inevitable from the beginning. ALL marriages and relationships should have a mission statement, and it should not be hidden away in some book stashed in the back pantry in the basement. Your mission statement should be beautifully inscribed on a large plaque of some sort and hung on your bedroom wall. It should be read by both husband and wife together, two to three times a day. It should be realistic and reflect both present day and future goals and plans; and it must invoke cohesiveness and patience for one another when traveling through both calm and treacherous storms. Before closing out this chapter, I would like to share me and my wife's mission statement:

As we embark on this journey hand and hand, we will not forsake nor turn aside from one another. God gave us to one another as an imperfect, yet unique gift. We will not fail him with ingratitude; we will please Him with a thankful heart, as He has found someone, besides Himself, that accepts me for who I am despite my flaws. I will love you unconditionally, and forever be there for you until death do us part.

A mission statement does not determine the integrity and longevity of our bonds to our spouses; however, the words contained therein should mirror the sincere intentions of both Husband and Wife. We must understand that we are bonded to one another for eternity, until that day when our souls are returned to the Creator. Please reflect on the following Bible passages and call them to mind in both troubling and kind times in your marriage/relationship; do enjoy:

> -*Ephesians 4:2-3: "With all humility and gentleness, with patience, bearing with one another in love, eager to maintain the unity of the Spirit in the bond of peace."*

> -*Colossians 3:14: "And over all these virtues put on love, which binds them all together in perfect unity."*

> -*Ecclesiastes 4:9: "Two are better than one, because they have a good return for their labor: If either of them falls down, one can help the other up. But pity anyone who falls and has no one to help them up. Also, if two lie down together, they will keep warm. But how can one keep warm alone?"*

> -*Mark 10:9: "Therefore what God has joined together, let no one separate."*

> -*Ephesians 5:33: "However, let each one of you love his wife as himself, and let the wife see that she respects her husband."*

> -*Ephesians 5:28: "In the same way husbands should love their wives as their own bodies. He who loves his wife loves himself."*

WHY WOMEN HATE TO LOVE

Why is it that women are now so reluctant to love, or fall in love, with a man? Whatever happened to man and woman living happily ever after? In this chapter, I hope to address why women hate to love and provide a broader perspective into some of the answers pertaining to this topic.

First, let us examine a few things. We all know that God created man for woman, and woman for man. What we don't know is why they (man and woman) cannot seem to live together according to the purpose and intentions of their Creator. What happened to the peace and solitude that was once experienced by the two beings? Why has it become so difficult now, for man and woman to relate with one another and understand each other? It must be very painful for those women who try so hard to keep themselves from falling for a man. I say that because a woman's nature compels them to find a man that they can truly love and devote themselves to, a man that she can trust and depend on to protect and comfort her that she may give freely and willingly the treasures that are confined within the depth of her soul.

Before I continue, let me be clear on one point, I do not in any way want to give the impression that all blame should be placed on the shoulders of all men. My intention is to share with each reader, whether male or female, a different and unique view of the emotional and complex struggles that women face currently, interpreted through the eyes of a man. Throughout the years, I have heard the cries and witnessed the tears, the heartaches and heartbreaks of many women that had devoted their lives and had given everything of themselves to those whom they thought they would spend the rest of their lives with and came to find that their counterpart not only had different intentions, but was not as honest, devoted, and loyal as they promised to be. I asked a young woman once, why did women see all men as being no good or as they now say "dogs"? And her response was that every time a woman encounters another woman and has a conversation relating to men, at least one of them has a story to tell about how some man in her past had misused her and destroyed her trust in men. She said that every woman that she had ever known throughout her life has had her heart broken by a man. Women are now faced with a very unfortunate circumstance; and I say that because human beings are naturally, sexually, and emotionally inclined to the opposite sex. When sex and intimacy is experienced between man and woman, one of the two, or both, will eventually develop feelings for the other, and in most cases, it will be the female who will develop these feelings. Men can be sexually involved with a woman for a protracted amount of time without ever having an emotional connection. He may be genuinely attracted to her, but that's completely different from having true feelings. Mainly because pleasure was the motive from the beginning and first interaction. Women have come to a point now where they fear to love, but still have that emotional and sexual desire; they still crave the physical, emotional, and sexual attention of a man. So now, some or most women are found sacrificing their values by only accepting a sexual partner, void of the components that composes a real relationship out of fear of falling in love and developing true feelings, so that they can protect themselves from being hurt. The attitude is, "If I don't love, I can't get hurt," but in the meanwhile, they still have a partner to experience **some** of the pleasures of being with the opposite sex. The reality is that women love commitment and oneness; they love to have a man they can call their own, absent the worries of being hurt or betrayed. I have a deep concern for the sacrifices that women have now made just to seek a degree of fulfillment from a man. What will the next generation of young women be taught? Will they, too, have to grow up making these same sacrifices? How will they be taught to make a stand and accept nothing less than what they deserve? If this cycle continues, what will be the outcome 30 to 40 years from now?

These are serious questions that must be addressed, as we can no longer be in denial or ignore the duties that are imposed upon us as men and women. We must take that step in healing our women, and the first step in that process is to treat our women as they should be treated—like royalty. There are, however, some men that will treat a woman like royalty and make her feel secure and loved, and he will give her all his attention, but his intentions and motivations will be false and deceptive. These particular men understand how to deceive women through the way they treat them, and as a result, women are hurt more by these types of men. How does a woman know if the right man has come along if the wrong man is so good at pretending to be "Mr. Right"? The most feared men of all to women are the nice guys; the ones that are respectful, caring, considerate, and compassionate. These men are deemed "too good to be true." Where does love factor in to this equation, or rather, problem? Love is not just an element, emotion, or feeling; it is a realistic way of life. The Bible says that "*God is Love*" (1 John 4:8). That says that we cannot find love, know love, or even comprehend love without having a connection with Him that is the source of such a powerful force. God uses love to set peace and selflessness in the Earth. It is Earth's greatest embellishment.

Now, having said that, I have spoken to women that have told me directly that they hate love. I have even been told that love is the cause of so much hurt and pain, so the world would be better off without it. It is terrible that some have grown to hate that which God himself has offered as his most perfect gift to humanity, man and woman, husband and wife. It's a woman's nature to love and be attracted to beauty, but love has been made ugly and unattainable to them. To some women, love is unreal, only a word, a special word that can be used to arouse or "get you in the mood," as some would say. But, I say if love was practiced and understood in its truest form, a man would never betray his woman, lie to his woman, hit his woman, or turn away from his woman, and he would give his life for her. There is nothing in the world he would not do for his woman. Women need to see and feel what real and pure love is like. They need to know that they are the most beautiful of all God's creations, and to them, a throne is given for their majesty, and there is a king who will fight to earn her hand. Women hate to love because there is a divine, internal yearning that goes unfulfilled, relationship after relationship. Women hate to love because they don't want to love when they feel they cannot trust. With all the intelligence, degrees of knowledge, and success that men have attained, we still fail to see the bigger picture. The bigger picture is the divine and harmonious companionship shared by two people, that are imbued with the highest level of respect and love for one another that they treat each other as they would treat themselves; hence, they begin to become one. The two realize that running from mate to mate is sheer foolishness, the two understand that God created Man for Woman and Woman for Man. The two can feel the realness of one man loving one woman and vice versa, then falling in love with the feeling of being and belonging exclusively. They grow to realize that in an imperfect world a perfect bond and perfect union is not a hopeless dream or fantasy, but something worth struggling and working towards. A woman would make any sacrifice, for there is no distance a woman would not travel for her man. She is a gift from God with a merciful and fragile heart that should be cultivated, nurtured, and guarded by someone who loves her deeply.

Why do women hate to love? Those that have endured a broken heart before know how painful and devastating it is; it affects you for years. Just think about it, you are deeply in love with someone, and you make them the center of your life and everything revolves around that person, although that shouldn't be. God should be our one true center, but some of us do make the mistake of allowing men and women to become our center. I have a fictional scenario I would like use to illustrate a point I wish to make. Now, let's say you and your spouse have been married for eight years, and trust was never an issue. You have two beautiful children together, and you are emotionally and financially secure. You go places, you have fun, you share secrets; you couldn't have asked for a better life. Then, out of nowhere, you gradually notice little changes, but you ignore them. You begin to feel like your companion is drifting away emotionally and sensually. You begin to ask questions but feel that the answers given are empty and unfulfilling. You can feel the lie causing confusion in your heart and mind but you ignore it and convince yourself that you're overreacting. Your feelings of unease continue and intensify to the point of it being impossible to ignore. So, you begin to hunt, search, and investigate; and what do you find? A phone number with a name of the opposite sex, and you have no idea who this person is. You present your evidence to your spouse, and he/she gives a riveting explanation. You entertain the idea of being a little paranoid. Later, you come across more evidence which is a lot more compelling and clear that your spouse of eight years has been dishonest and has betrayed the union. What do you do? You ask yourself, "Do I stay? Or do I leave?" Most often the second question is, "Why? Why did he/she do it? What made him/her do something like this?" Other questions follow, such as, "Does he/she still find me attractive? Am I not doing something emotionally, physically, maybe even spiritually to satisfy him/her? Does he/she love me anymore?" Your life was once beautiful, full of goals and aspirations. You viewed life in a positive way, waiting to overcome the next obstacle life throws at you, and you were ready so long as you had your partner, your counterpart, your friend, your dearest companion. The grass outside used to be green; now, you can't stand to look at it. Now, the sun is either shining too bright or it's not bright enough, and you really don't care to be around people as much anymore.

What happened? Your world came to an end; you are no longer an optimist. The pain was so severe that it gave your mind and soul a complete makeover. You have now even become dull and cold inside; you set up a defense barrier around your heart of great fortitude. You make a vow to yourself that you will never taste such pain again. What person would want to experience something so painful and distasteful again? The effects of this experience result in a lengthy phase of emotional and mental bitterness. It has been proven that recovery and the ability to move forward is possible, but this experience will shape and mold the victim, oft-times influencing future relationships.

Let's take some time to think and be rational; if we understand basic principles, we are able to comprehend complex principles and variations of experiences that influence thinking patterns and belief systems. Have you ever been betrayed, mislead, deceived, or abused by a police officer? Have you ever been betrayed or mislead by a confidant? Was the betrayal experienced on more than one occasion? How did you feel about them afterwards? Did it damage your trust and faith in dealing with an officer of the law? Do you feel reluctant and cautious of confiding in those that consider themselves to be your friend? Have you ultimately come to the realization that there is no such thing as a true friend? We know that people are different and embody different characteristics and different degrees of quality in their personalities. However, it is our overall experience and relationship with them that forces us to create opinions, feelings, and a lasting disposition that carry over into future encounters. Although it may have been only one police officer you had a bad experience with, the potential to develop a deep distrust for all police officers is possible because of that past encounter that left you with a scar physically or mentally.

Men must recognize that when they hurt the women that love them, they change her for the worst. The severity of the wound is based upon the magnitude of love she has for the one that hurt her. If the man in her life was her world and the center of her existence, the extent of her pain is unimaginable. Again, the Creator should be our center. Men, we break hearts as if a heart has no value and means completely nothing. We shatter lives; we ruin dreams; we damage and destroy the very essence out of which love emerges in women. We move from victim to victim, from house to house, ill-intentioned from the very beginning. Shouldn't we as men consider the feelings of the woman we share our bed, home, bad times, and good times with? Oft-times a woman will let the man she is involved with know what page she is on and what kind of relationship she is looking for. Most women understand the importance of clarity and motive when involved in something as serious as a relationship where two people's feelings are involved. To women, the sacredness and vitality of a relationship is high priority and extremely important. Most women will go above and beyond to keep all the high points high, and make a determined effort to elevate the low points in the relationship. I have spoken to a multitude of women, and the most repeated utterance embraced by them is, "If you find a good man keep him, and do whatever you have to do to keep him." They cook, clean, dress up, make up, give in, submit, compromise, and bend over backwards to please us, in an earnest attempt to show that their love is pure, true, and exclusively ours. Many women have found themselves being taken for granted after providing this kind of treatment. Women want to know why is it that when they give men what men complain they are neglected of, it seems to result in them being misused and taken for granted. What is it about us as men that when we find a woman that does not hold back her feelings, love, and desires to please us, we are so quick to abuse, disappoint, and overlook her? Some men will mistreat this type of woman, leave her and get involved with another woman that is the opposite of the one he left; and treat her as he should have treated the previous woman. What's wrong with us men? Why is it that when we have a great thing going we still aren't satisfied? These questions sound a little elementary, but the current state validates the questions and gives them relevance.

What happens when you put rotten foods and fresh foods together? You will find a chemical and physical imbalance in this equation that will result in the deterioration of a product or food that was once whole. When you put fresh foods with fresh foods they help to maintain and preserve one another, therefore adding to the longevity of its existence. Women have developed a rotten, and corrupted attitude from dealing with the foolishness of men. Women are tired of men, or so-called men. Could it be that women are now turning toward themselves, seeking relationships with other women out of disgust and anguish from their experiences with men. I once asked a woman her view on what she thought was the main cause and gratification of women being with women, and her response was that "a woman knows what another woman wants and needs." She also stated that the average man will never be relationship or marriage material. This is sad and deeply disturbing, as women are rapidly losing faith in us as men. It is in a woman's nature to turn toward her man for security, comfort, and compassion, to hold her at night and provide her with a love that is unique, unlimited, and unconditional. The credibility of men has diminished so much that all the natural desires (physically, mentally, and spiritually) that women instinctively rely on their counterpart to fulfill, some have now resorted to other women to satisfy. Not all women have resorted to this lifestyle because of this reason, as many have their own personal feelings and motivations that are completely different than what was previously stated. But to those that have turned down this road in search of true love and a true companion because of the lack of "real men," I want to be the first to say, I'm sorry. A young woman once said to me "Brother... I want a good man."

I cut her off and said, "Good is mediocre. When describing a real man, good is insufficient. We have the potential to be great men, magnificent men, extraordinary men. Being a good man is having a job, paying the bills, rearing your children, providing your family with the basic provisions of life, then a little extra. But a great man, an extraordinary man builds institutions and corporations for his family; he establishes his queen on the highest platform of physical, emotional, and spiritual security. An extraordinary man isn't just faithful, he's intuitively, divinely, wholeheartedly committed to his woman, without a spark of doubt in his mind that she is all the woman he desires, despite her flaws. An extraordinary man, when he is not able to provide a need or want at a particular time, goes out and uses the love in his heart for his woman and children to make away and satisfy their needs. An extraordinary man rears his children, cultivates his children, and teaches his sons how to relate to women and how to treat women. He is an example to his daughters of how a real man looks and treats his woman."

She replied that an extraordinary man in today's time is unheard of, and that if she could just find a good man, that would be extraordinary. I told her that there are extraordinary men out there that embody all of the above said and more, but I understand that some women have never encountered this kind of man. Some men believe that manhood dictates promiscuity and deception. Some have come to believe that when a man respects a woman and treats her according to her true value, that man is either weak or improperly taught. But an extraordinary man does not let what others think or say obstruct him from doing what he knows to be right. When a man desires a multitude of women for sexual pleasures, does this desire come from that bright and divine side of his nature? When a young boy desires to be a pimp, a player, and an abuser of women when he gets older, where does that desire come from? It is sad to see our young boys idolizing so-called pimps and players and women abusers. These young men just cannot wait until they step on the scene to show how good and gifted they are at acting out and personifying these ungodly roles. It's shocking to learn how prevalent this mentality is; we will find our most successful and intelligent men living these lifestyles, using their success to beguile and dupe women into thinking they are different from the player type. Real men just don't do these types of things. Women fear to love men, something so natural and right.

Why do women hate to love? I have associates, and friends that are involved in somewhat solid relationships. They have an almost perfect thing happening but still have other women on the side. All the while, their wives and girlfriends have absolutely no clue of the magnitude of betrayal they are victims of, nor would they even imagine it. Therefore, most women are shocked and devastated when they learn of such things because they never see it coming, and even afterwards, they still can't believe it. I give my advice and consistently suggest monogamy, and of course, I'm categorized as being weak, crazy, and stupid for having just one woman… silly me. Of all the characteristics that any man may possess, honesty is one of the most valued among women. When a woman knows that she has the kind of man that will remain true, honest, and faithful under all and any conditions, she feels more secure and at ease. Your woman will not believe that you possess these qualities because of your verbal proclamation of them; she gradually learns over time that you possess these qualities through your constant demonstration of them. Men, when your woman knows that you are weak in the moral department, the honesty department, and the maturity department, she doesn't trust you to leave her side for a second. She is reluctant to believe that you can be away from her for a protracted amount of time and do what's right. How does she know that you are weak in these specific departments? She watches you when you're not watching you. She looks at how you deal with everyone else; your friends, family, even mutual associates, and she begins to balance out the equation with the thought in mind that how you deal with the world is how you'll deal with her. We as men can be so arrogant to expect our women to believe that even though we lie to the rest of the world, we would never lie to them. This is not natural; our own nature compels us to relate and respond to all that we encounter according to how it functions. The underlying fact is that lies are spread and told by liars; and when we learn that someone lies or has told a lie, we don't necessarily pass judgement and rule them out a perpetual liar. But, the damage of a lie lingers for quite some time, always reminding the recipient of the lie that the giver of the lie does not always tell the truth. So, if a husband tells his wife he's going to hang out with "the fellas," and he has lied to her before, she understands that there's a possibility he may be lying again. But, she may still trust him because a woman truly desires to trust the man she loves. In concluding, I want to make a call to ALL men! Below are 10 "Dares" that I challenge every man, even those that are currently married, to meet and overcome—not temporarily but permanently. If you cannot overcome these small feats, you must ask yourself, "Am I really a man?"

1. I dare you to be honest and upfront in all your dealings with your her
2. I dare you to give your all to fulfill every promise made
3. I dare you to love with actions more than with words
4. I dare you to remain faithful and steadfast in your commitment to her
5. I dare you to deal with her with compassion
6. I dare you to study her to understand her better
7. I dare you to be patient with her in times you don't understand her
8. I dare you to always find time for her
9. I dare you to elevate and protect her
10. I dare you to let her grow into the woman you desire her to be

Till Death 4: Lost In You

My love, I'm so lost, deeply lost in you,
An endeavor that I long to forever last,
I'm enlivened by the taste of your lips in the evening,
I'm calmed by the strength of your grasp.
It says to me that you will never leave me,
Till death, we are lost in each other,
Till death, I am lost in the depth of your soul,
My heart could never find rest in another.
Most loyal, I am to my one and only love,
Against the world, I would stand at your side,
To give my life for you, the greatest of any pleasure,
Thus, is my measure, and till death, I'll abide.
I love being lost in my one and only love,
And what could cause me to stray from this bond?
I say nothing but death, for with you I am safe,
Our love will last till death and beyond.
What in the world is more beautiful than a bride and her groom?
What's more enchanting than a groom and his bride?
Till death, by your side with each passing moon,
To give both balance and ease to your stride.
I cry at times, knowing I could have been better,
My only desire was to serve you perfection,
A perfect love, a perfect warmth in an imperfect world,
To be lost with you in any direction.
As we dance into the realm of our quest to be one,
Each glance in the mirror shows me your reflection,
I'm lost in you, my love; I dare any to try and find me,
So consumed in the walls of your affection.
With each passing gaze, each smile shares a tear,
Knowing that our time is till death,
And that death will come, be it far away or near,

And one day, only one of us is left.
Till then, my love, I will cherish every second,
In this journey as I walk with you,
"Till Death," the words etched on the walls of my heart,
Till death, I'm so lost in you.

OF YOU

It's been many days since I've heard your voice;
My soul cries out for one touch.
Though you already know, it's a joy for me to say,
I care for you and love you so much.
So often, I think of the times we shared,
The smiles, the laughs, the tears,
And you never gave up; you stayed by my side.
You helped us get past the years.
My heart and your heart both share one beat,
If one stops, what good is the other?
You are a gift from heaven; you're God's greatest diamond,
And you're mine, I couldn't dare find another.
From sun up to sun down, my mind thinks of you.
At night, I cry out from my soul.
With you, the coldest nights always felt so warm;
Without you, the warmest nights feel so cold.
How bold am I if my eyes cry constant?
Am I a man if I deny what I feel?
Am I really a man if I decided to lie,
And tried to conceal what is real?
You are beauty perfected; it's a pleasure of mine,
To walk with you throughout this life.
You are my queen, my joy, my everlasting smile,
You are more than what it means to be a wife.
I just want you to know that you are precious to me;
I will never let go of our love.
Always know that my heart belongs to you,
Always know that you're all I think of.

LOVE SPELL

I am caught up in your love.
In the deepest of spells.
Your presence is accompanied
by the sweetest of smells.
I wonder sometimes
If falling could go any deeper;
In love with you is a privilege for me.
My God, I found a keeper,
A seeker once sought with a burning desire
To find the true mate for his soul.
Now, look at us two, bonded by love;
The beauty of two halves made whole.
Unfolded like a flower by the rays of the sun,
You amaze me as I stare in your eyes;
I never thought I would possess a possession such as you.
I'm obsessed, and I confess, I'm surprised!
I am caught up in your love spell; it is heaven to me,
A jail from which I'd hate to be freed.
My love, believe me once, believe me twice, for I am sure.
Forever more, your love is all I'll ever need.
An angel to my eyes, you caress my inner thoughts
And quench my longings for a perfect life.
Your perfect ways, your perfect smile, your perfect heart, your perfect mind,
All combined, how did I find the perfect wife?
Deeper in love I am with you,
Than the depths of the ocean's floor.
Of all the pleasures that life has to offer,
Your love is all that I yearn for.

FORBIDDEN LOVE

Our forbidden love, much like forbidden fruit…
Why should something so sweet be undone?
If I were to stand before God and He disagreed,
I would swear to Him that you are the one.
Our forbidden love, are we all alone?
Who else in the world understands?
If they knew we only wanted a picture painted perfect,
Then why do they despise our plans?
Oh, my forbidden love, with sorrow I write;
With tears, I try to explain.
With a heart full of love for the one I'm denied,
My pride now subsides in pain.
Forbidden, you are to my flesh and my soul,
A burning desire that shall last.
From my youth, I will carry this love till I'm old,
Lord knows, I will cling to our past.
I reach out to you from the confines of my heart;
You are established within the walls of my mind.
I think of you constantly. Oh, the times we shared,
These days, if I could, I would rewind.
Oh, my forbidden love, come walk once more.
Let's hold hearts as we soar through those days;
I was glue, and you were paper. Although our love is forbidden,
I will remember our love in those ways.
My forbidden love, sweet indeed you are;
The beauties you possess surpass many by far.
Your love is my sunshine; your eyes are my stars.
Your love is my sunshine; your eyes are my stars.
Wherever you are, or wherever you may be,
Forbidden love, I will love you for all eternity.
Forbidden love, our love means half the world to me;

The other half, we must conceal, that the world may never see.
I have a beautiful flower; you are a garden of roses.
You are a goddess, though I have a queen;
I have beauty and perfection combined and entwined,
Still, you are the best that I've seen.
You are my forbidden love; I have a love that's granted.
I have a diamond, but you are my sun;
If I were to stand before God, though He may say no,
In my heart, I know that you are the one.

ROSES ARE RED 2

Roses are red, violets are blue;
My dear, my heart belongs only to you.
Without you, my love, what in the world would I do?
It's true one is good, but better is two.
Me and you shall walk through these days and years,
My rose, with your petals, I shall wipe your tears.
My rose, if I have you, what fears will I know?
Lord knows I will hold you, and never let you go.
Roses are red; you are a violet as well.
From the Earth, you were created, but from heaven you fell;
Like a majestic blue, you embellish the skies.
My prize, your form is forever fixed in my eyes.
In your hands lies my heart, each beat only shows,
That each day, I love you more, for each day, our love grows.
My rose, my flower, my diamond, my star,
The other side of the world, if that's where you are,
I'd come, for you, far away is not far.
I love you so much; you own my soul.
Our hearts are like lock and key.
I cherish each second, each minute, and each hour…
You mean more than a lot to me.

ROSES ARE RED 3

They say the petals of a rose are the keys to its beauty,
And the magic is found within the flower.
They say a ruler is not a king without the heart of a queen,
Not in his army, but in her lies his power.
Each hour that passes, I fall deeper in love
with the rose that I have known from my youth.
It's been so many years; I watched you grow.
From day one, I loved you forsooth.
Roses are red, and violets are blue;
My life without you is like a dream untrue.
What force could undo these vows that we have taken?
When the world is too much, you're the one I run to.
So delicate and soft, your beholders are amazed.
My rose, your beauty's one of a kind;
My rose, we're getting older; I love you more each day.
If you do have any flaws, my love is blind.
Roses are red; violets are blue,
Both our hands are entwined.
Roses are red; violets are blue,
Let's do the same thing with our minds.
Within you, my rose, I find a greater joy.
I look forward to our life and many years,
And if I had to live this life without my one and only rose,
I'm sure I'd live a life of many tears.

WITHOUT YOU

Without you, what am I
But a leaf without a tree,
A heart without a beat.
Without you, there is no me;
I couldn't walk this earth alone,
So, my love, please take my hand.
With you, I am an ocean with unlimited treasure.
Without you, I am a grain of sand.
Without you, I am lost, and darkness is home;
Crying out to find you, the farthest I roam.
What in the world could compare
To a love so sweet?
So complete is my life,
It was destined we meet.

THE BOOK OF ME

I have reached a page that I don't want to read;
I don't know if it's the middle or end.
I have come to the part where I must make a decision
That will determine if I lose or win.
I remember the days when I was just a young boy;
I would have never guessed this future of mine.
Oh, what I would give to revisit those days,
To once again relive in that time!
All of my love and hate, but most of all my love,
Makes me hate this life that I own;
The love of my life, the one I love more than life,
Both of which I wish I had never known.
So, now where do I go? What shall I do?
I pray I don't make a mistake,
My Father, please help me, 'cause I'm all out of answers;
I don't know which road I should take.
I wake up in the morning and creep to the mirror;
It's a shame I can't look at me.
I open to the page that I refuse to read,
At the end in the book of me.

THE BOOK OF ME

I fantasize of an old man in a rocking chair,
Staring out into the field of days,
Smiling and wondering how I made it through,
All the pain brought about by my ways.
I never expected to make it this far,
Who could believe this would happen to me?
I couldn't conceive in one billion years,
That my strife would allow me to be.
My heart will always be with the ones I've hurt,
May God be with those that have passed,
I hold my head back a little and look at the sky,
And thank that God is my friend at last.
My well has dried up, I can cry no more,
Throughout this book, I have lived the pages,
I know I've done wrong; you reap death for sin,
I'm still here, but I've paid the wages.
I fantasize of an old man in a rocking chair,
I hope that's how this story will end,
Only 26 years in the book of me,
Watching time disappear like the wind.

PAIN

Such pain I feel when I think of you,
Our love is now a thing of the past.
So fast those days decayed into naught,
I thought that our love would last.
Now I'm so hurt, lonely, and bitter,
So lost and so cold inside,
I cried last night, and the night before,
I love you, to hell with my pride!
How does one overcome such a feeling?
Is it possible to heal such a scar?
How is it possible to embrace another heart?
When I only wish to be where you are.
Only you can free me from this prison,
Only you can put an end to this pain,
If we were not meant to be, then why is it so,
That without you, my mind goes insane?
We only live for a short while indeed,
And I'd rather spend that time with you,
Every fleeting moment and forsaking hour,
Becomes eternity when I'm with you.
Does not God understand that I love you?
Does He not care that I need you?
You are my heart and soul, the very air to my lungs,
How could He not know that I breathe you?
Thoughts of you just torture me,
Thoughts of us hurt even more,
I don't want to think; I want you here in my arms,
Why can't it be like it was before?
I just want you to know that I love you,
My future envies my past,
I will never accept the goodbyes of those days,
I thought they would always last.

This Soul

This soul seems so strange,
This soul confuses me,
I wonder if I abuse this soul,
Or if this soul abuses me.
This soul has made me cold,
This soul just makes me cry,
And if this soul was made from truth,
Then why does this soul lie?
This soul has been given wisdom,
This soul has been given light,
This soul has been taught,
The origin of wrong…
So why isn't this soul right?
This soul will suffer dearly,
This soul will pay for its sins,
This soul will be condemned to divine pain,
If this soul does not make amends.
This soul has been blessed beyond greatness,
Why does this soul choose left?
But still with this soul, I pledge to thee,
With every moment's breath.

NOBODY

Although I am known, my soul is kept sacred;
In darkness it dwells alone.
No woman, no man, no judge can judge
This heart or this soul that I own.
No one knows me;
No one can imply, or give an opinion
Of what lives inside.
If I laugh, I know the world will laugh with me;
If I cry, then I'll be forsaken.
So, I'll keep my laughter, and I'll keep my tears,
And live on until my soul is taken.
But who's pure enough to glance at me
With sleek or slanted eyes,
And condemn me for all my worldly sins
And the tongue that spread my lies?
I am conscious of the wrong I've done,
But who's conscious of all I've done right?
Why is it the world can remember all of my wrong,
But leave my good deeds out of sight?
Nobody knows my soul,
So don't waste your time
Trying to judge my soul, my heart,
And my mind.

ALL BECAUSE OF YOU

In my world, the sun never ceases to shine.
They say love is rare; in my eyes love is blind.
My heart is content, so is my soul and my mind,
AND IT'S ALL BECAUSE OF YOU.

I see roses and violets, but you are my flower;
Your presence is required each second in an hour.
At times, I grow weak, then I'm inspired with power,
AND IT'S ALL BECAUSE OF YOU.

When I am riddled with pain, your hands caress me;
When I am filled with passion, your hands undress me.
I am filled with hope when life's trials suppress me,
AND IT'S ALL BECAUSE OF YOU.

Down the darkest road, I travel with light.
When I feel there is none who understands my plight,
I am relieved and strengthened to carry on through the night,
AND IT'S ALL BECAUSE OF YOU.

Though the stakes are high, and the odds are vast,
I have the faith and the vision to look forward and past
To see the rope of sweet victory within my grasp,
AND IT'S ALL BECAUSE OF YOU.

When this life is complete, I will lay down and smile;
You made all these years so worth the while.
With joy, I encountered every day and every trial,
AND IT'S ALL BECAUSE OF YOU.

2GETHER

As we lay in still darkness,
I feel the warmth and the beats of your heart.
My rose, you have the eyes of the rarest diamond;
Stay with me without one moment's part.
These days of ours are bound to end,
For no soul can live forever.
With love these days will become eternal,
So eternally, we'll be 2gether.
Will you grant me to call you,
My angel of years?
Of all the tears I've cried
And of all my fears,
Losing you was the one thing
my heart could never bear.
Me without you, I would liken to
Someone trying to live without air.
Hold my hand; lets walk 2gether.
Let me whisper in the ears of your mind
It's a beautiful feeling; I love being lost,
Understanding that love is so blind.
As we lay in still darkness, staring in each other's eyes,
I tickle your spine with a feather.
Stay with me without one moment's part;
Let us always remain 2gether.

THE BOOK OF ME

It's been so long;
I still watch the sun rise,
And I watch my son grow,
Wiping the tears from his eyes,
So soon to be a man.
Time flies so swift;
"Time waits for no man,"
I unbrand it, a myth.
So many things, I have seen,
So much pain to behold,
And through the heat of the darkness,
They keep saying to be bold.
They advised me to stand up
When I was already standing,
Then I decided to sit
When to stand was demanding.
I cease to inquire
What the end shall be;
I now beg my Lord
To be a friend to me.
What makes me go this way?
Why don't I fear
The wrath of the great
That brought me here?
And now, here I am, just look at me!
Only 23 pages in
The book of me.

THE BOOK OF ME

I know some wonder
If there is any good to tell;
They yearn to hear words of heaven,
Since they so often hear words of hell.
I write from where I stand;
I'm driven by mind and state
With actions I write on the papers of time,
And on paper, I write of my fate.
My soul holds the answer,
And I myself demand
A reply for things unknown,
Things I don't understand.
My eyes are red; my head is heavy;
My hands are disappointed with me.
They build, and they build, yet nothing possessed,
Even though I was anointed to see.
I love my Lord; He is my shepherd.
I left, but I want to come home.
I ask that He help me
Through the trials of my future
And make my past unknown.

FORBIDDEN LOVE 2

Forbidden love, where are you?
Tell me, why do you make me cry?
I had a dream we were engaged in a kiss,
That painful kiss called goodbye.
Forbidden love, I can't live without you;
Forbidden love, my heart is so sore.
I can't eat, I can't sleep; forbidden love, I'm confused.
Tell me, what is our love forbidden for?
Forbidden love, I've tried to move forward;
Without you, I must wear a mask.
Forbidden love, you are a jewel that only I should wear,
A flame that only I could grasp.
If I should die tonight, it would be so relieving,
'Cause I can't live this life without you.
And I don't want to live, for I will never enjoy
These days or these nights without you.
You are a never-ending melody, a delightful tune,
Truly the rarest of any kind.
Forbidden love, you own my heart;
You own my soul; you own my mind.
Always know that I crave you,
And that I love you with all of my soul.
Forbidden love, without you, this heart of mine
Will never again become whole.

TILL DEATH 2: BY THE FIRE

This craving of mine, an unquenchable desire,
A cup to be filled by my heart's only fire.
So still, we lay, in my mind, I see forever,
And if time disagrees, please deem time the liar.
Through your eyes, I encounter the beauty of your soul;
Together in this life shall we grow young, not old.
Till death, I will hold and console this bond.
We are no longer two, but two halves made whole.
Your hurt is my hurt; my joy you can take.
I delight in watching you sleep at night,
Till morning, till the moment you awake.
As we sit by the fire, your hand in my hand,
Our hearts, warmed by a love the world fails to understand,
Exchanging soft words that emerge into a kiss;
Our dreams, so plentiful like grains of sand.
Without up, there is no down; without two, there is no three.
I can't live without you; the truth is, my love, without you there is no me.
This life without you has no purpose or worth;
If you leave, this form will return to the earth.
My love, with the breath I was blessed with at birth,
I searched for you, determined to possess you first.
If ever there were a flower to spend a day just glancing,
At you, with you, my heart will spend all day romancing;
Let us lose ourselves as we sit by the fire,
Engaged in such passion that neither fades nor tires.
Till death, we are tied and entwined with such strength
That surpasses eternity and defies any length,
That conquers any heights and dares to soar higher,
So inseparable our embrace, till death: by the fire.

STILL ALIVE

So blessed I must concede, able to breathe another hour,
Able to quench another thirst, plant a tree or pick a flower.
So many souls were laid to rest, I stop to think and stare;
I know my number was called, but someone said of me to spare.
What have I done? What will I do? Is this life in need of me?
Or am I in need of life? What am I blind to that I must see?
My confines were once the womb, and now, this world just seems too small.
To and fro I travel, though there was a time I could only crawl.
At times, I am so ungrateful for this gift my Creator gave.
What could it be? Why hasn't my soul gone to drift in the eternal wave?
So blessed I must concede, able to hold my love much longer
Able to wipe another tear, and when life's too heavy, to be much stronger.
I ponder at times and think to myself in the darkest room I can find,
In the deepest part of my mind these rapid years, I try to rewind.
I watch time sift through my fingers like tiny grains of sand,
And I'm thankful for each and every moment I'm granted to roam this land.
This marvelous Earth, such a beautiful creation, two eyes could ever behold;
The mysteries of life, such beautiful secrets, two ears could ever be told.
So blessed I must concede, able to open my eyes at dawn,
Able to see the sun once more when there are those forever gone.
To grow in wisdom, things so obscure become so clear to me,
To enjoy the scent of a rose I hold such things so dear to me,
The buzzing of bees, the chirping of birds, and the calming smell of rain;
Such things I'll miss when in that day the list contains my name.
I know, one day, the nature of life will cause this form to lay.
I'll still be thankful; I'll go in peace, though every part of me will want to stay.
These eyes of mine; this mind, indeed, loves in depth the breath I breathe.
So blessed I am, I must concede, to both laugh and cry, love and grieve,
To count the stars, or follow the sun as it creeps across the sky,
Wanting to be the best in all that I do, but fall and continue to try.
So blessed I must concede, able to open my eyes at dawn,
Able to see the sun once more when there are those forever gone.

THE ROAD

Long and suffering, with no relief in sight,
Though wrong, at times, I extend to death an invite,
If I might, for a day, to lay down the load,
Evading the pains, by forsaking the road.
Some days, I cry, because it's all that's afforded,
And every day, there awaits a new trial.
Oh, how I wish, for my good deeds to be rewarded,
To exchange all my frowns for one smile.
I sit and wait awhile, each mile hoping for a friend.
Will it stop? Though I hope not for the road to ever end.
I've passed by many, both strange and familiar faces,
Family that I'll never see again.
I cry out to my Lord for understanding and patience,
And wings that I may soar through the pain.
In my eyes, I see sunshine when the skies cry out with rain;
When the joys of life forsake me and only doubt and fear remain,
I travel the road in both darkness and light.
I shouldn't, but at times, I extend to death an invite,
To take me away, to grant freedom to my soul,
To deliver me unto hands that will heal and make whole.
I'm determined to keep forward as I travel the road,
"Going back is not an option," I once was told.
My older me once said many years ago,
That days such as these would arrive,
The younger me was in denial, the younger me disagreed,
And rebelled with all the strength he could derive,
At length, I am tired, yet I continue to fight.
It's not right, but at times, I extend to death an invite.
I loathe that I travel the road alone,
I've seen many, but on whom can I rely?
I've been embraced, yet I feel true love is unknown,

And those closest are the ones that defy.
As I continue onward, I embrace the bitter,
And endure till this journey's complete.
They say you reap what you sow; it's true, I know.
I pray my Lord to be a light unto my feet,
As I walk through the darkness of the road ahead,
With desires to live and go aright,
I know, yes, I know, that no soul should ask for death.
Still at times, I extend to death an invite.

I Promise...

I promise to be your rainbow in the midst of every storm,
Big or small, short or tall, I'll take you in every form.
My eyes see only beauty when they gaze in your direction,
I promise I'll always love you with a heart of unyielding affection.
I promise to be your sunshine for tear drops and for rain,
Your blanket when you're cold, your medicine when in pain.
If you find yourself alone in this world, I'm asking you to look once more;
I promise you forever, I'll be your strength when you're too weak to endure.
My hands are at your mercy; you can use them at your will.
For days that have no ending, or quiet nights restless and still,
All and anything that's mine, there's nothing I would deny you.
If the world leaves you standing alone, I will always stand beside you.
Through the darkest storm, I'd follow, and brave the waves of any trial
It matters not how long to me, be it eternity or only for a while.
I promise a promise of limitless love, and faith as pure as gold;
I'll watch you from sunset to sunrise; you are the greatest sight to behold.
As long as the sun shines, as long as birds chirp, and a bee sucks nectar
from a flower,
I promise to love you each second in a minute, and each minute that lives
within an hour.

TILL DEATH 3: THE JOURNEY

Till death, my only love, on a road that never ceases,
On this journey to rebuild whatever's broken,
On the way there will be tears, most of joy and some of weeping,
Thoughts that should have been shown or at least spoken,
Till death do us part, your heart is safe with me.
So beautiful, this union of two,
With this ring I thee wed, forsaking all, and this world,
For the world, I will discover with you.
There's nothing more glorious than two separate souls,
On a quest to make two halves into one perfect whole.
One Bride, one Groom, two hearts, two tunes,
Two hands, one enclosed in the other.
One road, one journey, and if we both get tired,
To survive we must carry one another.
Two lovers, two doves, two stars worth watching,
You complete me in unimaginable ways.
You fit perfectly into me; I am your lock, you are my key.
Let's shine; you be my sun, I'll be your rays.
Let us drink from a fountain that's endlessly sweet;
From the core of my being, I promise till death.
The day God decreed it was destined we meet,
Though I finally found you, I had lost my breath.
I had lost my step, though my balance was complete,
The day God decreed it was destined we meet.
You are my perfect friend, the only mate for my soul,
I'd follow you to the depths of the deep.
We can soar through the heavens in the depths of our thoughts,
Or share dreams and subtle kisses while asleep.
In the darkness of the night, I'll add brightness to your light;
When you're lost I'll be the lamp that guides your feet.
Through heaven or hell, by your side, I'll abide
Your companion till our journey's complete.

So Precious

Indeed, I proceed to construct a song for her,
With the most enchanting melody unknown to ears.
I awe at the majesty enforced by her nature,
And I behold the crown that she has worn for years.
So, so precious, I title the song,
With words that are ingrained in passion;
The very essence of her soul, I must concede,
Is the meaning of love everlasting!
I deem it a blessing to witness her smile;
Such a joy just to catch her eye.
Though awake, I lay dreaming all the while,
Begging time not to pass me by.
So, so precious I title the song,
With words that are rich with truth.
I predict that when she reaches old age,
She'll be just as beautiful as she was in her youth.
All the diamonds of the Earth could never equate,
Nor compare to just one glance.
So, so precious, and to this song,
I beg of her just one dance.

THE LETTER

Did you get the letter, the letter I sent?
You should have gotten it yesterday.
In it, I explain what I really meant;
I don't want you to go, please stay.
The letter I wrote was not long, nor short,
Nor did I write it in vain;
It was just enough to express my love for you,
As well as rid you of your pain.
Please take me back; I won't hurt you again.
I know I've made promises before.
This time, I will show and prove my devotion;
I'll be all that you desire, and more.
In the middle of the letter, I said something like,
"You are worth more than all silver and gold."
At the end of the letter, I said,
"Over the years, you were a flower I watched unfold."
I hope that you'll read it, and if you deny,
You'll break my heart in two.
I'd drown in my tears, oh, yes, I would,
Just by being apart from you.

MISERY ME...

I had her heart in the palm of my hand,
What a fool of I to let it slip away.
Misery me, I'm branded forever,
I took her granted, what more can I say?
I'm reminded of the wise man that tried to lead,
I'm the dumb man who's lost and confused.
I asked, and he told, he told, and I asked,
Though I knew not, I still refused.
How does one let go of such perfect love,
Without a justified reason to give?
And if one was truly and deeply in love,
From then on, how does one manage to live?
Her heart was like an ocean, and I was a sailor,
Traveling both calm waters and force.
And both I expected, I knew what I was facing,
So how then did I fall off course?
The other day, someone called me by my original name,
And I replied, "I'm just misery me."
He said, "Why would you call yourself such a terrible thing?
I know not such a thing you to be."
I said, "My heart and my head are both burdened with sorrow,
And my soul is emerged in guilt,
For whom do you know of to destroy a kingdom
That by his own hands were built?"
Without her, I am fallen to no more again rise;
This is so clear to visibly see.
Give me all of the riches of the world, without her,
I'm still miserable misery me.

I'm Sorry

I'm sorry I didn't make it when you called and asked
If I could be there to cheer for you;
It hurt me deeply, and I hope you believe
That I care about what's dear to you.
I'm sorry I didn't come the day I promised I would;
There is no excuse I could give.
I want to make another promise: from this point on,
I'll be there for you as long as I live.
I hope you don't hate me; I hope we're still friends.
Please don't take your smile from me.
I could be at work, at church, in school, or asleep,
Just call for me, and I'll come see.
I thought I knew everything, but now I see
That there's always room to learn more.
I'm not a man of greed; I don't want everything;
It's just your body and your mind I yearn for.
When I look in your eyes, I see heaven perfected.
When I touch you, I feel perfect inside.
It took a lot for me to write this; I've never done it before,
But for you I'd swallow my pride.
For what it's worth to you, I hope you value these words.
I'm sorry if I let you down,
And most of all, I'm sorry if I ever was the cause
Of that beautiful face of yours to frown.